GREYHOUND

A Pictorial Tribute to an American Icon

GREYHOUND

A Pictorial Tribute to an American Icon

ALEX ROGGERO

WITH TONY BEADLE

OSPREY
AUTOMOTIVE

First published in Great Britain in 1995
by Osprey, an imprint of Reed Consumer
Books Limited, Michelin House,
81 Fulham Road, London SW3 6RB and
Auckland, Melbourne, Singapore and
Toronto.

ISBN 185532 548 9

Editor: Shaun Barrington
Art Editor: Mike Moule
Design: the Black Spot

Printed in Hong Kong

OVERLEAF *The inimitable Clark Gable and Claudette Colbert in Frank Capra's 1934 Oscar winner,* It Happened One Night. *This comedy about a runaway heiress and an opportunistic journalist exploited the romantic plot device of an escape across country, courtesy of Greyhound, to the full.* (Columbia: Courtesy Kobal)

The montage pictured on page 9 was created by Andy White.

All contemporary photographs by Alex Roggero apart from page 47, courtesy Hyman Myers. Captions by Alex Roggero. Main text by Tony Beadle.

to Carlo and Louise

For a catalogue of all books published by Osprey Automotive
please write to:

The Marketing Department, Reed Consumer Books,
1st Floor, Michelin House, 81 Fulham Road, London SW3 6RB

ACKNOWLEDGEMENTS

This book would not have been possible without the knowledgeble assistance of many dedicated and professional Greyhound employees. My warmest thanks go to all the drivers, station managers and service-crew members I had the pleasure of meeting during my time on the road. Special thanks must go to Amy Engler and everyone at the Dallas depot, as well as the managers of Evansville IN, Cleveland Ohio, Uvalde Texas and Jackson MS terminals.

As anyone who has taken a Greyhound trip will know, a bus journey is as much about meeting people as it is about going from A to B. During my travels I got to know hundreds of fellow passengers. I thank each and every one of them for their time, and wish them all a happy journey.

Of the many people who helped during the course of my research, I am indebted to architect Hyman Myers, of Vitetta Group in Philadelphia, for providing the pictures of the restored Washington terminal.

I am also grateful for the support of Karen and Richard Spector, who provided invaluable archival information and helped organize several bus trips. American Airlines' generous assistance made a number of research trips possible, therefore making a huge contribution to the project.

Many thanks also to everyone at AutoCapital magazine in Milan, especially Gilberto Milano and former editors Luca Grandori and Filippo Piazzi, for supporting my 'road' articles and photography over a period of several years.

In London, Rosie Thomas, Steve Brookes, Andy White and Matt Prince gave leads and ideas and supplied all kinds of materials, whilst Ceta West End processing lab took care of the colour transparencies with their usual effortless competence. My gratitude also goes to my editor, Shaun Barrington, for giving me the time and freedom to represent Greyhound's past, present and future exactly as I wanted.

Thanks are insufficient to acknowledge the role played by Jacquie Spector Roggero, also a photographer, who was instrumental during the picture selection process and provided tremendous support throughout.

Finally, and for reasons that have to do with photography, design and the romance of the road, I would like to acknowledge the influences of Russell Lee, Alan Hess, Jack Duluoz and the old favourite, my 'American' globe-roaming grandpa.

Alex Roggero

I would like to thank the following people who provided extremely useful help and information for this book: Ed Stauss of *Bus World*, Woodland Hills, California; Nick Georgano; Kit Foster; Nicky Wright; Amy Engler and Betty Haynes in the Public Relations Department of Greyhound Lines Inc, Dallas, Texas.

Tony Beadle

CONTENTS

FOREWORD
Spirits of the Road

It all started on a rutted mud track, a single lane road between two small mining towns in Minnesota. In a sense, it could not have happened any other way. Even then, in 1914, what was to become the Greyhound empire was based on a simple but visionary idea: the necessity to link America's myriad communities with an efficient and inexpensive transportation network. In the country where to be without wheels was a symbol of second class citizenship, there were millions of people, living in thousands of towns, who had no wheels. The Greyhound bus gave them mobility, that quintessentially American commodity, and turned them into coast to coast travellers.

Over the course of many years the bus, with its conspicuous aluminium and stainless steel body criss-crossed the nation, knitting together those communities, embedding itself deeper and deeper in the American psyche. So much so that in the end it became another symbol for the country itself, like a Coke bottle or a pair of Levi's. But unlike these objects, the Greyhound was more than a typically American product. It was a mobile icon, a travelling receptacle of people's dreams and people's problems. Its silver sides reflected, like a mirror, many big and small events that shaped American history – from the pioneering days of road building, when the Greyhound routes were inaugurated almost as quickly as the

new highways were opened, to the engineering advances of the thirties, when Greyhound buses were the first with rear-mounted engines, the first to use diesel, the first to have on board air-conditioning. And then there were the buildings, the network of impressive streamlined terminals, with massive towers and multicoloured neon signs.

Greyhound was one of the first US companies to realize the importance of what is now described as "the corporate image". Its impact on American society was such that it came to be reflected in all facets of popular culture. In 1934 Frank Capra's Oscar winning movie, *It Happened One Night*, romanticized bus travel for the newly affluent middle classes, while at the same time blues singers such as Robert Johnson and Lee Brown dedicated entire songs to the Greyhound, the vehicle of escape for many Southern blacks on the way to a better future up North. In the post-war years 50% of all intercity travellers went by Greyhound, and the Silversides became a symbol of the nation's unprecedented wealth and desire for travel. The Beats discovered the bus and immediately fell in love with it. Jack Kerouac's *On the Road* became an inspiration for generation after generation of incurable road romantics, for whom the great American landscape, geographical and spiritual, was best observed from the widescreen windows of a Scenicruiser. During those golden

years the Greyhound bus even managed to accommodate two very different sets of people: those who went searching for the American Dream, and those who rejected it.

But it could not last forever. Inevitably, the years that followed were not so golden. Competition from airlines and privately owned cars as well as periods of economic recession made life increasingly difficult for the old Greyhound. In 1983 the deregulation of the airline sector forced the company to implement a massive programme of pay cuts, which the drivers reiected. The resulting industrial dispute turned out to be one of the most intractable in US history, and has only recently been fully settled. The Greyhound image has also changed. What was once a symbol of the future appears to have turned into a photograph from the past. The bus, redolent of a gentler, more relaxed America, now has to survive in a much harsher environment. Some of the magnificent terminals have become stranded in the middle of deserted and unsafe downtown areas, while economic pressures are forcing the company to close many secondary routes.

In this climate of striking contrasts, where the old Greyhound myths are constantly buffeted by the realities of modern American life, I decided to board a coach and, like many photographers, writers and movie makers before me, take a ride that lasted several thousand miles. It was a journey of rediscovery, in the sense that I went looking for the old buses, stations and signs that helped create the Greyhound myth, as well as a contemporary exploration, in that I wanted to document bus travel in its present form. To my surprise, I found much of Greyhound's glorious past still intact, and much loved by both staff and passengers. But perhaps the most striking feature of the trip was the realisation that the bus is one of the last public spaces in America where people from very different backgrounds are still willing to interact. In a country where people's attitudes are often polarised by class, colour, gender and language, this seems to me to be a major achievement. The ritual begins with a simple question: "Where ya headed?" The answer can last twelve hours. The fact is that in the last 80 years some things at least haven't changed. If you want to get to know America's soul, to put your finger on its pulse,and experience the sense of community that makes total strangers talk for hours on end there is, still, only one way to go.

Alex Roggero

VACATION PLEASURE
in DOUBLE Measure!

CROSS the continent twice—by different routes, if you wish—and see BOTH the New York and San Francisco World's Fairs . . . all for $69.95 total transportation cost! Your ticket is good for three months, so you can stay as long as you like or stop off en route to spend the night, visit friends, or go sightseeing. With scientifically planned air conditioning to keep you comfortably cool . . . deeply cushioned, reclining chairs . . . and wide, clear windows, you'll find your trip the most pleasant ever. Friendly fellow-passengers add to the interest, and frequent schedules provide maximum travel convenience. See your Union Pacific or Interstate agent for information!

Visit BOTH Fairs for only $69.95

MAIL COUPON FOR FREE FOLDERS

Paste this coupon on a penny postal card and mail to Travel Dept., Interstate Transit Lines, Omaha, Nebr. (Check information desired.)

☐ San Francisco World's Fair
☐ Western Wonderlands
☐ New York World's Fair
☐ Other points of interest

Name

Address

City   HT-639

Cool and Fresh
as a mountain top

Cool vacations begin the moment you step inside an air-conditioned Interstate or Union Pacific Super-Coach. Gentle no-draft circulation keeps the air clean, fresh and invigorating throughout the trip.

INTERSTATE TRANSIT LINES • UNION PACIFIC STAGES

INTRODUCTION
America's 'Silver Bullet'

My first experience of travelling by Greyhound was in October 1974. In those days the Toronto bus depot was in the heart of downtown, only a block or two away from the Holiday Inn where I had squandered far too many of my pitifully small roll of precious dollars on a bed for the night.

I had tried to catch the bus the previous night and sleep on board to avoid the hotel bill, but my flight from England had been delayed and I arrived too late to catch the daily departure heading west to Winnipeg. Clutching my 'Ameripass' in my hand – good for one month's unlimited travel in the USA and Canada – I entered the vault-like building and approached the dark wooden ticket desk in one corner. As it was fairly early in the morning (a combination of jet lag and trepidation at being alone in a strange country had prevented much sleep) the queues at the windows were pretty short and soon I was able to exchange the pass for a sheaf of tickets.

There were a few hours to wait before my bus was called and I spent some of the time just watching the comings and goings as the depot grew busy – the hustle of the passengers, the bark of the diesel engines, the announcements of buses arriving from, and departing to, cities I had only dreamed of: New York, Montreal, Detroit, Chicago – but most of all I marvelled at those wonderful, gleaming, stainless steel and aluminium machines painted in red, white and blue with the sleek greyhound along the sides.

I climbed aboard eventually, and as instructed by friends back home who had done this sort of thing before, took the window seat in the second row on the opposite side to the driver. The theory was that during the day you got to see out of the front, but at night could duck down and sleep without being bothered by the headlights of the oncoming traffic (it works pretty good, too!).

As we headed north out of the city I still wasn't sure what to expect. My destination was over 1,300 miles away – an amazing distance to travel by road for someone brought up on an island less than 600 miles from top to bottom – I would be on the bus for more than 30 hours, and yet I still wouldn't have reached the middle of the country!

Long distance travel by Greyhound soon develops its own rhythm as the road disappears beneath the big wheels at a steady pace, the scenery slipping effortlessly by like a never-ending travelogue, and the small towns passed through quickly fading to be forgotten. You look out of the window, read a few pages of a large book bought especially for the journey (in my case Tolkein's 'Lord of the Rings') or talk to fellow travellers. Then, every three hours or so, there's a longer stop to change drivers which gives the passengers a chance to stretch their legs and grab some refreshment. I remember my surprise at the first such stop being told by the driver that I could reserve my seat by simply leaving my jacket on it, and my bag could safely be left in the overhead rack while the bus was cleaned and refuelled. Is that still true today I wonder? When the new driver took over, he was more in the mood to talk than his predecessor and I learnt that Greyhound pilots spent their time driving back and forth over the same stretch of highway, passing the bus along as if it were a giant baton in a relay race lasting for thousands of miles.

It was on the second day that I also began to understand just how important the Greyhound bus could be in such a huge country. Passing along the shores of Lake Superior the bus was flagged down by a young couple whose car had broken down – we were miles from the nearest small town and if it hadn't have been for the Greyhound they would have had to wait (probably for several hours as traffic was very sparse) for a passing motorist to rescue them.

My journey to Winnipeg was completed without any problems and after a few days staying with friends I rejoined the Americruiser heading west. Following the Trans Canada Highway (little more than a two lane blacktop in places) I visited Regina, Calgary, Edmonton and Vancouver before heading south to my ultimate destination – Los Angeles, California.

Riding the Greyhound bus in Canada in '74 was a great experience. Air travel was still relatively expensive and the railways had somehow lost their glamour, so it seemed that everybody used the bus: students, families, old people, military personnel, children – it was a cosmopolitan and popular form of transport.

The contrast when we crossed over the border into the United States was immediate. The bus was now for those who couldn't afford a car. The first person who sat next to me as we headed out of Portland, Oregon, hadn't shaved for a while and his opening gambit was to try to 'borrow' some money for a phone call so's he could contact his relatives when we arrived at Salem in an hour's time! Looking back, it is easy to see the problems that were mounting up for Greyhound in the 1970s. Their depots were often run-down and in undesirable locations in the poorer areas of cities and on long distance routes they were facing increasing competition from the airlines. For local travel, people were using their own automobiles and the bus company was undoubtedly feeling the pinch.

On reflection, my journey across Canada was probably as close as I could have got to travelling by Greyhound in its heyday of the '50s and '60s. And the importance of the bus to rural communities in those days cannot be overstressed – Greyhound shipped parcels and freight as well as people across the country. For thousands of small towns across America, the bus was an essential lifeline.

I vividly remember one stop in the middle of the prairie. It was nothing more than a crossroads with a small diner on one corner, and no other building in sight as far as the eye could see in any direction. The main highway stretched from horizon to horizon in an unbroken line and it was over an hour since we had passed the last signs of habitation. As the bus pulled up I counted six pick-up trucks parked outside the cafe. Four passengers got off the bus and were driven away, two new passengers joined and the last remaining pair of pick-ups disappeared. After a few minutes, when the dust had settled, it was hard to believe there had been anyone there at all.

Other images, just as striking, remain with me over twenty years later. Sunrise in the Rocky Mountains; toast, jelly and coffee in the diners (my staple diet); sentry-like grain silos standing alongside the railroad tracks; the driver arguing with a pedestrian who had walked in front of the bus as he pulled out of the depot; a row of tennis balls dangling from the roof of one depot to guide the bus drivers into their parking bays; and many, many other delights of that journey of discovery between 13 October and 7 November 1974.

There isn't a single photograph of my trip; I had deliberately not taken a camera with me because I didn't want to be looked upon as a tourist. Such a vain and foolish youth...

Tony Beadle

A COLD START
Hupmobile to Greyhound

No one man invented long distance bus travel, and the idea of transporting passengers for a profit in America predates the invention of the automobile by over 150 years. The first regularly scheduled public stagecoach line opening in New Jersey in March 1732, when Solomon Smith and James Moore advertised that they were going to operate two wagons between Burlington and Amboy, a distance of fifty miles. Although some local citizens expressed fears that the speed of the eight-miles-per-hour wagons would make them a danger to other road users, it is not recorded how much discomfort the passengers endured on the journey.

In 1756, a stagecoach line ran for the first time between New York and Philadelphia, taking three days to complete the route, travelling for 18 hours a day. Commissions from Congress to carry mail helped boost stagecoach lines, but it was still an arduous means of long distance travel – in 1785 Weddale Stage Lines took six days to go from New York to

LEFT In 1914 Carl Eric Wickman, a Minnesota car dealer, bought for $600 a seven passenger Hupmobile, like this one, and changed the course of US transportation history. He used the car to transport miners from the firehouse in Hibbing to the town of Alice, ten miles away. The ride cost 15c one way and 25c round trip, but it was worth it: Alice had the best saloon in the area. The little bus was an instant succes, and eventually it evolved into the last great American whales seen in the background.

ABOVE *Hibbing to Alice: the first seeds of an American icon.*

Boston, along rutted and dusty tracks. Journey times began to come down however, and by 1831 Washington to Philadelphia could be done in five days; but on the eastern seaboard the stagecoach was facing increasing competition from the burgeoning railroad systems with their steam powered locomotives.

Out west nevertheless, the stagecoach was still the only method of passenger travel available, and on October 7, 1858, a big Concord coach (of the type seen in the western movies) drawn by six horses, arrived in Los Angeles, California, 20 days after leaving St. Louis. Carrying only five passengers and a small amount of letter mail, the Overland Mail Company's stagecoach did the 2,600 mile marathon non-stop – running day and night – crossing deserts, the vast plains and even going through hostile Comanche Indian territory along the way.

The legendary stagecoach company of Wells Fargo was formed in 1852 by John Butterfield, Henry Wells and William Fargo and in 1868 they were granted a government subsidy for a daily, cross-country mail service to California. But the completion of the transcontinental railroad the following year foretold the end for stagecoach travel over long distance routes.

While the railroad was infinitely better than the stagecoach, it did have one major drawback – the trains could only travel where there were tracks laid down for them. Horse-drawn coaches were still in demand for local journeys and there was even a special type of vehicle developed for getting people to the railroad – called a depot hack or station wagon.

The demise of the horse as transport didn't happen overnight, and although Charles and Frank Duryea produced the first US-built gasoline powered motorcar in 1892, it wasn't until 1903 that an automobile crossed the continent. That car, a two-cylinder, six horsepower Winton, took nearly two months for the drive from coast-to-coast, but had demonstrated the capability of the new fangled 'horseless carriage'.

Development of the automobile in America proceeded at a frantic pace, and soon there were hundreds of companies in the business of constructing motorised vehicles. Most of these were hand-built, and therefore expensive, and it was only when Henry Ford introduced his famous Model T in October 1908 that owning a car started to come within the reach of the working man.

It was around this time that a young Swedish immigrant

ABOVE *Aerodynamics not a priority in 1914.*

Thrill to *ALL* of
CALIFORNIA

Above left: Fabulous Treasure Island is now brilliant with color and excitement as San Francisco's Golden Gate Exposition thrills thousands of gay visitors.

Above right: There is always something exciting going on in fascinating Hollywood. Here is a movie première!

ENJOY GREYHOUND'S
Nite Coach Sleeper!

Here is the pleasant and enjoyable way to travel to and from California ...the Greyhound Nite-Coach sleeper. By day you can relax in a soft, comfortable seat, at night, you can stretch out in a full-length berth. Each compartment of the Nite-Coach contains a wash basin, running water, space for clothes and a radio. Two lavatories and a ladies' lounge are likewise available. Beginning June 1 (Eastbound) and June 3 (Westbound) this service will operate daily between Kansas City and Los Angeles. (Extra berth fare $4.50 single and $6.00 double.) Make your trip to California, or between Los Angeles and San Francisco ($1.00 Berth Fare), this luxurious convenient way.

FOR COMPLETE INFORMATION WRITE NEAREST GREYHOUND TRAVEL BUREAU

920 Superior Avenue, Cleveland, Ohio

12th and Wabash, Chicago, Illinois

917 McGee Street, Kansas City, Mo.

905 Commerce Street, Fort Worth, Texas

560 S. Los Angeles St., Los Angeles, Cal.

Pine & Battery Streets, San Francisco, Cal.

GREYHOUND

arrived in the United States seeking, as did millions of fellow travellers, his fortune in this fabled 'land of opportunity'. Carl Eric Wickman ventured as far west as Arizona, where he worked for a short time in a saw mill; he then moved north to Hibbing, Minnesota, where he was employed as a drill operator in an iron mine. Job security in the Mesabi open-pit mining business was non-existent, and lay-offs occurred quite often. When available, the work was dirty and hard, and the hours were long, but the pay must have been pretty reasonable because, when he left the mines in 1913, Wickman was able to buy his own business – a dealership for Hupmobile cars and Goodyear tyres – located in Hibbing.

As any automobile dealer would have done in those days, Wickman also undoubtedly ran a taxi service in and around Hibbing. The story goes that, in 1914, when a new Model 32 Hupmobile touring car was proving difficult to sell, Wickman paid $600 to buy the automobile for himself and began using it to ferry miners from Hibbing to Alice, a distance of ten miles. Seven miners could be crammed into the Hupmobile,

From little acorns...Following the success of the Hupmobile (above) the Mesaba Transportation Co. was formed in 1916 when Wickman was joined by Ralph Bogan, Arvid Heed and Dominic Bretto. By 1918 the company had a fleet of 18 buses and a route system that covered most of Minnesota.

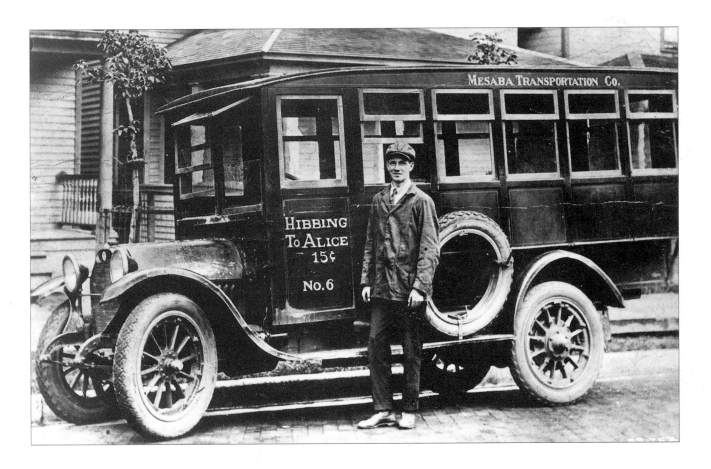

each paying a fare of 15 cents for a one way ride, or 25 cents for the round trip between the firehouse in Hibbing and the Alice saloon over rough and rutted roads. From this tiny beginning was to grow the huge Greyhound bus network that eventually covered the entire North American continent.

However, the notion (largely promoted by Greyhound) that Wickman's fledgling enterprise was the first intercity bus route in America seems to be inaccurate. As early as October 1907, W.B. Chenoweth was operating a service between Colorado City and Snyder, Texas, using his own design, six-cylinder 'motor driven stage coach'. Chenoweth's venture was short-lived, mainly due to passengers being wary of his unusual vehicle and, when a local cattleman purchased four

Buicks and went into direct competition, his fate was sealed.

As far as can be ascertained, the first successful, regularly maintained, scheduled intercity bus service began on 1 March 1912 between Luling and San Marcos, Texas. The operator was Josh Merritt who converted a 1906 Packard to carry up to seven passengers and their luggage.

In these early days of course, there was no such thing as a bus. The vehicles used were, like Wickman's Hupmobile and Merritt's Packard, ordinary cars that were sometimes modified to carry more people. Local taxi services expanded the territory they covered and developed routes between towns, forming into small intercity transport companies – but many of these soon fell by the wayside.

Meanwhile Wickman's Minnesota operation was booming, thanks to the iron mines working at full capacity to meet the demand created by the war in Europe, and he soon brought in a partner to help share the driving chores, A.G. 'Bus Andy' Anderson. In 1916, the Mesaba Transportation Company was formed by a merger between Wickman's company and Ralph Bogan's taxi company that plied the route between Hibbing and the 'big city' of Duluth. The newly formed organisation had a fleet of five cars and five drivers on the payroll. In that first year of 1916, the Mesaba Transportation Co posted a profit of $16,000 – a tidy sum in those days.

An important step in the history of intercity bus travel also came about in 1916, with the introduction of the Federal Highway Act in July of that year. President Woodrow Wilson gave his full backing to the legislation which sought to bring

The Gray Line Motor Tours, Salt Lake City, Utah.

Main Office and Starting Point, The Newhouse Hotel.

In 1928 and 1929 Wickman's organisation acquired several bus companies that bore the name "Greyhound": Northern Greyhound, Southern Greyhound and Eastern Greyhound Lines used comfortable, reliable coaches such as this Z-250 (below) built by The Yellow Motor Coach Co. of Chicago, Illinois, a subsidiary of General Motors.

about the much needed improvements required to the U.S. road system and, in so doing, helped speed the development of bus travel.

By 1918, Mesaba Transportation had expanded to an 18 vehicle fleet with a network of routes that covered a large part of Minnesota. Then, in 1922, Carl Wickman sold his interest in the company and moved his family to Duluth, where he took on the task of organising bus lines to complement the train

services of the Great Northern Railway rather than compete with them. Forming the Northland Transportation Company, in four short years he helped build up a system that he was able to sell to Great Northern for $240,000.

This sale had two effects. First, it created an interest in the idea of the railway companies owning bus lines and, more importantly, it gave Wickman and his associates the where-withal to begin creating their own system – one based on the

ABOVE *The Mack bus was one of the best of its time. The state-of-the-art six-cylinder gasoline engine produced plenty of power and the bullet-style shock absorbers efficiently dealt with the bumpy roads of the day.*

BELOW *The first Greyhound Company logo was a blue shield that incorporated the name, a stylised dog and a drawing of the Mack. In later years, as different models were introduced, the bus drawing was dropped.*

ABOVE *An American institution was officialy born in 1930, when Greyhound Lines Inc. was formed. The newly named company had over 1800 buses travelling the nation's highways. The magnificent, specially designed Mack bus arrived in 1931, having been vastly improved since its inception in 1926. Built by the famous Mack Truck Company, it offered unprecedented speed and comfort and was used primarily – not surprising in the light of the cost – on the newly opened transcontinental routes.*

notion of small, independently owned bus companies getting together in large, regional affiliations. In September 1926, a holding company called the Motor Transit Corporation was formed by Wickman, Ralph Bogan, Orville Caesar and E.C. Eckstrom. Basically the new enterprise came from the partnership between Mesaba Transportation and Eckstrom's Safety Motor Coach Lines which operated out of Chicago and also served much of Michigan.

It is from E. C. Eckstrom's Safety Motor Coach Lines that the name 'Greyhound' seems to have originated, although his company was not alone in using this descriptive identification. Eckstrom apparently settled on the name after hearing a passenger say that his buses ran "like greyhounds". Coming at a time when bus companies were looking for more zappy trade names to create the idea of speed and comfort, and in so doing promote the advantages of travelling with them, it was a natural. After a short while, Safety Motor Coach Lines started using 'Greyhound Lines' as their operating name.

As soon as it was up and running, the Motor Transit Corporation started making acquisitions, the first in 1926 being Interstate Stages which ran buses between Chicago and Detroit. The division of responsibilities between the four men at the top of MTC seems to have been fairly clear-cut: Wickman and Caesar provided the day-to-day operations

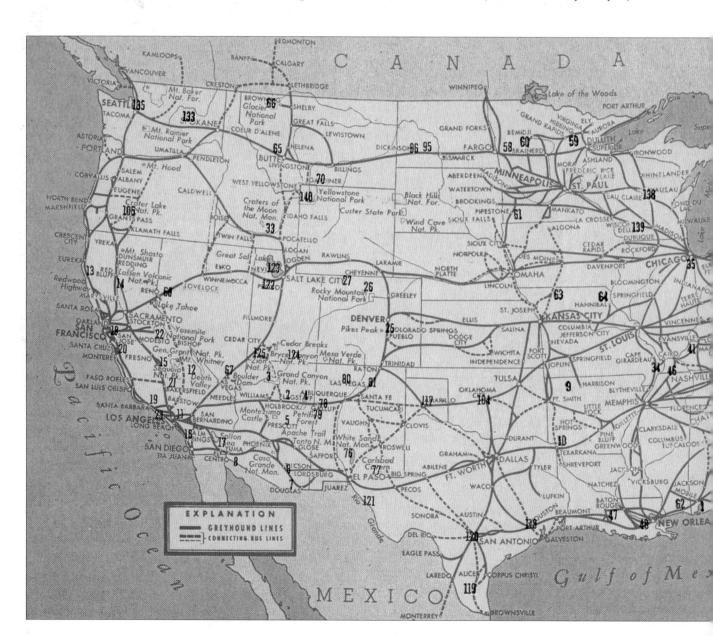

LEFT *The typical 1930s Deco interior lights on the Mack allowed night-time reading and the thick cloth side curtains kept sun and dust at bay. In those days there was no air conditioning.*

BELOW *The 1931 Mack bus was amazingly comfortable, even by today's standards. The seats were covered in pure Massachusetts mohair, with horsehair stuffing. For kids or last minute passengers there were special flip-up seats that made intelligent use of the aisle space.*

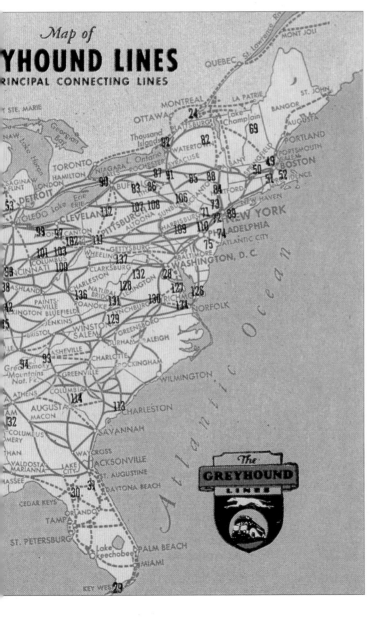

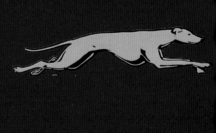

REYHOUND L

KANSAS CITY ST LOUIS CHICAGO CLEVELAND

"FOR BETTER SERVICE"
all AMERICAN
BUS LINES, Inc.

★★ RED STAR MOTOR COACHES, Inc. ★★
SALISBURY, MARYLAND

management skills, Eckstrom handled the promotions and advertising, while Bogan searched for potential take-over candidates. However, cash was still in relatively short supply and it was only the arrival of Glenn W. Traer, an investment banker from Chicago, that got things properly in motion. Traer had purchased a large tranche of MTC's first stock issue and resold it at a profit, and he was therefore able to arrange loans and establish lines of credit to support the growing company.

By 1928, a dozen different companies were amalgamated in the MTC 'Greyhound' system, with some 325 buses on the road. Aggressive marketing of the period using the Greyhound name is typified by a newspaper advertisement of the Southland-Red Ball Motorbus Company exhorting businesses to get their salesman to use the bus instead of driving a car. Touted as being a third of the cost of a private automobile, the 'Greyhounds of the Highway' were said to be 'the most economical means of transportation available'. The slogan 'Ride The Greyhounds' is repeated in many other similar advertisements, firmly establishing the public's awareness of the name.

1928 was also the year that a bus completed the trip from San Francisco to New York in 5 days and 14 hours. Leaving the west coast on September 5, the bright yellow Pioneer Stage bus, belonging to the Yelloway System of W.E. Travis, was the forerunner of a transcontinental service operated by the American Motor Transporation Company.

East of St Louis the route was run in conjunction with other independent companies, as AMT had yet to reach that part of the country.

Northland Transportation, the company started by Carl Wickman in 1922, became Northland-Greyhound Lines in 1929 when Motor Transit Corporation bought

ABOVE RIGHT *It's difficult to imagine now just how snappy this rig must have looked back in 1930; and it doesn't look all that 'quaint' today.*

ABOVE *Early Greyhound coaches advertised on their flanks the main cities covered by the network. A coast to coast trip cost around $55.*

LEFT *The twenties was all about 'rationalisation' for the MTC Greyhound group. Logic dictated that the myriad tiny bus companies across the country would begin to amalgamate.*

In the days before streamlining (or more accurately, before it was taken seriously for everyday, workhorse machines) coaches looked more like trains than buses. The Mack's brakelights were indeed railroad lamps. Baggage was stowed on the roof and had to be secured very firmly in order to avoid dangerous shifts when the bus had to negotiate tight bends.

a part interest. But this was only a tiny part of the Greyhound expansion going on in that year. In February 1929, MTC paid a reported $6 million for American Motor Transportation and in so doing, not only removed the threat of Yelloway encroaching on their territory in the mid-west, but also opened up the California routes to Greyhound.

At the same time, the Greyhound network was spreading rapidly in other directions too, with MTC working in co-operation with the wealthy railroad companies to add more bus companies and more routes to their system. The eastern sector, taking in Pittsburg, Philadelphia and New York came into the fold via a link-up with the Pennsylvania Railroad which evolved into a jointly owned operation, Pennsylvania Greyhound Lines.

With the name Greyhound proliferating in such a rapid manner, it came as little surprise when, in 1930, the Motor Transit Corporation officially became Greyhound Lines Inc. That same year, the corporate headquarters were moved from Duluth to Chicago.

Altogether, there were 3,520 intercity bus companies operating in North America in 1930, with 14,090 vehicles covering 318,715 route miles and totalling up an incredible 7.5 billion passenger miles. These were the Depression years of course, and Greyhound advertisements stressed the economical benefits of bus travel more than the (apparent) convenience and (arguable) comfort aspects.

During the process of expanding by buying up a number of small companies, the Greyhound 'fleet' inevitably consisted of a variety of different makes and types of buses. Famous names such as White, Fageol, Mack, Yellow Coach and others produced what were known in the 1920s as 'parlor cars' – which looked like stretched versions of the sedans available at the time – even automobile makers like Studebaker and Pierce-Arrow were in on the act. Often the bus companies themselves would produce their own bus designs by taking a truck chassis and adding a hand-built body that fitted their particular local requirements.

However, it is the Fageol Safety Coach which really set the early standards for intercity bus construction. Founded by brothers Frank R. and William B. Fageol in 1917, the Fageol

Motors Company of Oakland, California, started out making expensive luxury cars that were guaranteed to do eighty miles an hour – thanks to a six-cylinder, 125 horsepower aviation engine supplied by the Hall-Scott Motor Company. Demand for the big Fageol automobiles was extremely limited, and the company sensibly turned its attention to the manufacture of trucks and buses.

In 1921, Fageol produced what is probably the first ever American vehicle designed specifically as a bus. Low-slung, with four wheels and four passenger doors down the side (it would be a few years before the centre aisle configuration caught on) the 22-seater 'Safety Coach' proved immediately popular with operators and passengers alike. Competitors were quick to see the advantages of the design, and brought out their own versions, notably White in 1922. Fageol responded by stretching the wheelbase further and increasing the width of the body to accommodate 29 passengers.

Wickman and Bogan's Mesaba Transportation Co. used Fageol Safety Coaches on their busy route between Hibbing and Duluth in 1922, and the ever-widening Greyhound organisation obviously had many Fageol buses on its roster in the latter part of the decade.

By 1927, Greyhound itself was in the bus building business, thanks to the acquisiton of the C.H. Will Motors Corporation of Minneapolis, Minnesota. Early Will buses looked almost identical to the Fageol Safety Coach and were obviously copied from them, but gradually they became bigger, heavier and provided more luggage space. The final bus from Will was delivered to Greyhound in January 1931, thereafter they sourced a large number of their new buses from the GMC division of Yellow Coach.

It was during 1926 that Mack introduced a six-cylinder bus designed for long distance, high-speed use. By 1929 this bus had been considerably improved and the BC Model as it was

RIGHT *The details show the high quality of design and manufacture of the mighty Mack. A chrome greyhound sits on top of perfectly spaced engine air vents.*

called, now carried 29 passengers in some style. The central aisle did away with the need for a door for each row of seats, but interior luggage space was still fairly limited, and most of it had to travel on the roof rack. Mack also produced a six cylinder, 126 hp BK version until 1931, but thereafter the company cut back on interstate building, although production of the Mack BC continued until 1937 in small quantities.

At the start of the 1930s, the vast majority of intercity travellers who didn't use their own car went by train – over 70% in fact – while the bus companies handled around 25% of the passenger traffic. This was to change gradually throughout the period leading up to World War Two, with the bus taking passengers from the railroad and reaching a peak of a 35 per cent share of the market.

ABOVE *The practice of putting a shining chrome greyhound on the coach's front started with the Mack. This went on for many years and was one of the little touches that made Greyhound buses special. Sadly, the chrome emblem is missing from current models. Design is in the detail...*

LEFT *Going Greyhound: in the 1930s travelling became the new national pastime. People from every corner of the country flocked to the 1933 Century of Progress Exposition in Chicago, thanks to all-expense-covered Greyhound bus tours. Magazine ads proudly proclaimed "There is no better way to see America than the Greyhound way".*

ART DECO JEWELS
Station to Station

Survival was the name of the game for Greyhound in the early part of the 1930s and although its route coverage continued to expand as it bought up more bus companies it wasn't until the 1933 Chicago World's Fair – officially named the Century of Progress Exposition – that the tide began to turn.

Thanks to the amazing exhibition, demand for travel to the Windy City boomed, and Greyhound was ideally placed to benefit from the increase in passenger traffic to its centre of operations. Having been granted the exclusive on providing transportation inside the fairgrounds, Greyhound then took a huge gamble and reserved 2,000 hotel rooms for the duration of the Exposition.

In what was probably one of the first examples of the cheap 'package holiday', Greyhound then advertised all-in bus tours to Chicago. Anywhere in the USA, passengers could buy a ticket that would provide bus travel, admission to the World's Fair and hotel accommodation in one. The idea caught on and the tours were a sell-out, with many people making more than one visit to the event.

But if leisure travel provided a much needed boost to the income of Greyhound and other bus companies, it was the regular daily services which produced the 'bread and butter' revenue. Exactly how important the bus had become in rural America can be seen by two letters of support sent to the Texas Bus Owners Association in 1929.

J.E. Guthrie, Secretary of the Salado Chamber of Commerce, wrote: 'Years ago, Salado being an inland town, felt great need of a railroad. We no longer need one. We have six Greyhound buses each way in 24 hours. Our people like the service – the bus line fills a long felt want.'

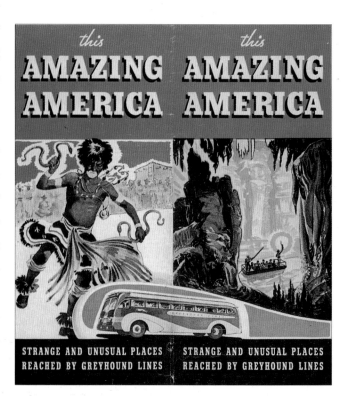

SWING AROUND AMERICA!

THIS SUMMER.. by GREYHOUND

Call it what you will—a fortunate conjunction of the planets, or the inscrutable march of events, *or just plain good luck*—but 1939 has brought to America the most amazing cycle of fun, excitement and thrills in its fast-moving history!

Shining stars in this galaxy are the New York World's Fair and the Golden Gate Exposition. But sprinkled between, on this giant coast-to-coast orbit, are the scarcely lesser lights of vacation enchantment—cool and wondrous national parks, northern lakes and mountains, surf-swept beaches, dude ranches, every summer scene on the map.

"I can't see them all in my short vacation, on my small budget," say you. But you can! That's where Greyhound steps into the picture, with the amazing rate of $69.95 to both Fairs and a hundred places of thrilling interest in between—over any route.

"But I simply can't take time to see both Fairs," you come back (wistfully). Well then—visit whichever Fair you've set your heart upon, throw in a cool vacation resort or two—and still save dollars over any other type of transportation that rolls, swims, or flies.

A great fleet of Greyhound Super-Coaches—streamlined, smooth-rolling, efficiently ventilated or completely air-conditioned—awaits your pleasure!

GRANDEST CIRCLE TOUR IN TRAVEL HISTORY— *visiting both Fairs . . .*

This amazingly low rate includes transportation from your home, across the continent to one Fair, then back to the other, and return to your home—following your choice of scenic routes. You can take as much as ninety days—or the trip can easily be made in two weeks. It's an all-time bargain, no matter how you plan it.

for only $69.95

Ask about Expense-Paid Tours . . . they save time and money, add pleasure, assure hotel reservations.

The GREYHOUND LINES

PRINCIPAL GREYHOUND INFORMATION OFFICES

Cleveland, O. . . . . East 9th & Superior
Philadelphia, Pa. . . . Broad St. Station
New York City . . . . 245 W. 50th Street
Chicago, Ill. . . . . . 12th & Wabash
Boston, Mass. . . . . . . 60 Park Square
Washington, D.C., 1403 New York Ave., N.W.
Detroit, Mich. . . Wash. Blvd. at Grand River
St. Louis, Mo. . . Broadway & Delmar Blvd.
Charleston, W. Va. . . 155 Summers Street
Minneapolis, Minn. . . 509 Sixth Ave., N.

San Francisco, Cal. . . Pine & Battery Sts.
Ft. Worth, Tex. . . . 905 Commerce Street
Memphis, Tenn. . . . 527 N. Main Street
New Orleans, La. . . 400 N. Rampart St.
Lexington, Ky. . . . . 801 N. Limestone
Cincinnati, O. . . . . 630 Walnut Street
Richmond, Va. . . . 412 E. Broad Street
Windsor, Ont. . . . 403 Ouellette Ave.
London, England
. . A. B. Reynoldson, 49 Leadenhall Street

THIS BRINGS PICTORIAL WORLD'S FAIR BOOKLETS

Mail this coupon to nearest Greyhound information office, listed at left, for bright, informational folders on NEW YORK WORLD'S FAIR ☐, or SAN FRANCISCO'S GOLDEN GATE EXPOSITION ☐. Please check the one desired. For information on any other trip, jot down place on line below.

Information on trip to _____

Name _____

Address _____ HT-6

1937 GREYHOUND SUPER COACH
NOSTALGIA ON WHEELS!

Yes, 1937 was a very good year. The San Francisco Golden Gate Bridge was completed and was the longest in the world at that time. The Greyhound Super Coach was also introduced, and was considered the "Ultimate in bus design."

Some of its features included...first rear engine bus — first with baggage compartment underneath — jump seat for the porter — first to be air-conditioned.

This bus was recently located in South Dakota where it was being used by a church. Greyhound decided to restore the Super Coach to its original condition in keeping with the current nostalgia trend and to preserve a little history.

Today, the 1937 Greyhound Super Coach is a vivid example of how much Greyhound Motor Coach travel has changed for the better over the decades — changes that have made Greyhound the number 1 motorcoach carrier.

1937 Super Coach. Greyhound was one of the first US companies to adopt the streamlined approach of the Art Deco era. Orville Caesar, Wickman's right-hand man since 1922, was responsible for the development of a revolutionary new bus, produced in 1936 by Yellow Coach of Chicago. Aptly named "Super Coach", it was full of innovations. For the first time in history, the engine (an 11.6 litre gasoline unit) was mounted transversely at the rear, thus increasing the number of seats to 37. This also allowed the creation of a luggage compartment underneath the passanger area, doing away once and for all with the fiddly and dangerous roof racks. The blue and white colour scheme emphasised the streamlined design and promoted an image of speed and efficiency. The significance of the Super Coach for Greyhound is indicated by this later advert, a perfect example of what Willie Davidson called "The New Nostalgia".

Jasper Chamber of Commerce Secretary, Ed C. Burris, was even more fulsome in his praise: '... it is not possible for an individual or group of individuals to estimate the importance of Bus transportation in Texas and the United States.' Burris went on to explain in meticulous detail: 'You take this town for an example, and I feel there are numerous other communities in which similiar conditions exist. We can depend upon the Bus service for more frequent means of getting about than the Railroad. This condition is not brought about by neglect of the Railroad but is made possible by six Highways radiating out of our little town. Each of these Highways accommodate from one to three Buses each way every day ...The Buses assist the surrounding communities in reaching our little city, for shopping and other business

Greyhound Bus Station, Evansville, Indiana

ABOVE Evansville, Indiana. As the Super Coaches criss-crossed the country and revenue came on tap, Greyhound went on a building spree. This resulted in a network of terminals of unprecedented beauty. The one in Evansville is internationally renowned as an Art Deco masterpiece. Designed by W.S. Arrasmith, it was completed in 1938, at a cost of $150,000. Over 100 buses were scheduled in and out of this terminal each day.

RIGHT A hand-painted 1939 view of Evansville Terminal.

ABOVE When Greyhound adopted Streamline Moderne as its company image, it did not fail to exploit the power of neon. All over America, terminals designed by the Louisvillle firm of Wischmeyer, Arrasmith & Elswick featured signs that would not have looked out of place on the Las Vegas Strip. In small towns like Evansville the Greyhound terminals lit up the sky, shining like beacons of modernity, harbingers of adventure.

LEFT The typically Deco central tower advertises the Greyhound name in vibrant red, while at the top the blue neon exercises the running dog. Although many terminals of the period featured a 'running dog' sign, this is the last working example left in the country.

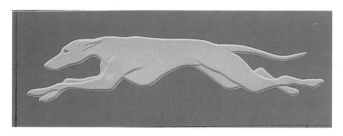

ABOVE *The blue and white colour scheme adopted for the Super Coaches was also used for the terminals. In this way Greyhound was able to enhance its corporate identity in city after city. The large glazed tiles and emblems are typical of these stations throughout the 1930s.*

purposes ... This manner of service could not be rendered by any other means of transportation.'

But it wasn't all plain sailing: whenever there was a big demand for transport (such as the Chicago World's Fair) then unscrupulous 'wildcat' operators would try to get in on the act. These rogue companies rarely published a list of fares or a timetable, and often gathered a vehicle load of passengers together for a trip on a 'cost sharing' basis. Some wildcat drivers even resorted to snatching luggage away from a rival bus line and loading it on their vehicles – a guaranteed method of getting the passenger to switch carriers. As the situation worsened, complaints from customers grew louder, bus companies and state regulatory bodies protested in unison, and this eventually resulted in the US Congress passing the Motor Carrier Act of 1935.

This act brought all bus companies engaged in running interstate routes under federal control, via the Interstate Commerce Commission. From now on, all bus lines operating across state borders were required to adhere to fixed schedules and tariffs. And, while existing carriers who were operating 'regular' bus services when the Act came into force were granted 'grandfather' certificates to continue in business, afterwards any company wishing to start up a new service had to apply to the ICC for a certificate.

Because existing bus lines could protest these applications, one effect of the Act was to limit the number of new companies able to enter the system. Another result was that, in certain cases, an existing bus line could gain a virtual monopoly over a route. In turn, the granting or holding of an ICC certificate became a valuable commodity, one that could be bought and sold.

Overall, while the ICC regulation was welcomed, it tended to accelerate the process of the preceding years of reducing the number of bus lines in operation – mainly by mergers. Altough Greyhound's expansion programme had been relatively dormant in the early '30s as the company looked to modernize its bus fleet and upgrade the facilities at bus terminals and garages.

However, in 1935 Greyhound set up an agreement with the New York Central railroad which led to the creation of the

ABOVE *More Evansville decoration. In those days attention to detail was such that even the door handles were something special. Each and every one was solid brass and decorated with the shield-type logo of the period.*

ABOVE *The Evansville Greyhound station is no museum. It still welcomes hundreds of buses every week, and each time Station Manager Joe Kaylor is there to help weary passangers down the steps, give directions and even unload baggage. Which makes this one of the nicest terminals to arrive at in all the network.*

RIGHT *Glass block – the construction material of the Deco era – is featured in most terminals of the period.*

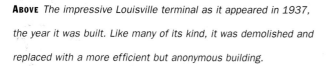

ABOVE *The impressive Louisville terminal as it appeared in 1937, the year it was built. Like many of its kind, it was demolished and replaced with a more efficient but anonymous building.*

Central Greyhound Lines of New York which operated between New York, Albany, Buffalo and Cleveland as well as many other routes. As a consequence, the existing Central Greyhound Lines that covered routes from Detroit to Columbus, Cinncinati and Louisville had its name changed to Ohio Greyhound Lines to prevent any confusion.

Because the Greyhound network had been created over a number of years by pulling together a wide variety of different companies, for any long distance traveller there were still some obstacles to be overcome en route. When changing from one line's area to another, often a new ticket had to be issued, and sometimes it was necessary to change buses – inconveniences that the passenger could do without.

In addition to its own extensive advertising in the press, Greyhound bus travel received some big boosts from Hollywood during the depressed years of the '30s. The first

film to prominently feature a bus as part of the plot was *Fugitive Lovers* from MGM in 1934. This was followed by *Cross Country Cruise* from Universal Pictures and then, arguably the most famous bus movie of all time, *It Happened One Night* starring Clark Gable and Claudette Colbert. This Columbia Pictures release created the impression that riding the bus could be exciting and might even lead to romance. Some twenty years later, the 1956 remake, entitled *You Can't Run Away With It,* starring June Allyson might have failed to

RIGHT *Hopkinsville, Kentucky. Compare the Evansville Terminal with one of today's anonymous bus stops. In some extreme cases, such as the one pictured here, the Greyhound "station" is no more than a small sign lost in a sea of other signs.*

America's "OUT-OF-TOWN CAR"

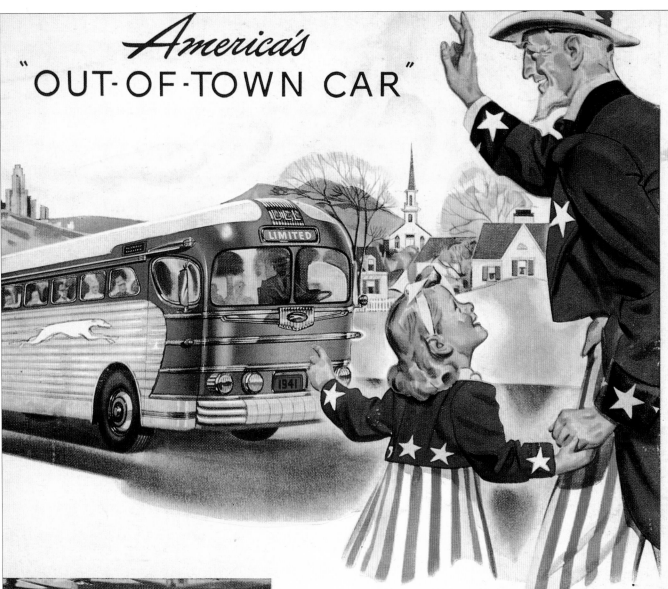

is the finest on the highways

—yet it costs less to ride, has the world's safest driver

● Millions of Uncle Sam's nieces and nephews are making their trips out of town these days in their *second cars*—we mean Greyhound Super-Coaches, of course! Why not you? You'll save a lot of wear and tear on your automobile—on your pocketbook—and on your nerves, too! These big "out-of-town cars" are warmed and ventilated like a pleasant living room—they ride as smooth as silk—and the men at the wheel are 14 times safer than the average driver! It's the pleasant way to travel on business—and you'll enjoy a business-like saving on pleasure trips! Fares are only a fraction of the cost of driving even a small car. *Try Greyhound—next trip!*

Principal Greyhound information offices are located at: New York City • Cleveland, Ohio Philadelphia, Pa. • Boston, Mass. • Washington, D. C. • Detroit, Michigan • St. Louis, Mo. San Francisco, California • Fort Worth, Texas • Minneapolis, Minn. • Lexington, Kentucky Charleston, W. Va. • Cincinnati, Ohio • Richmond, Va. • Memphis, Tenn. • New Orleans, La. Windsor, Ontario, (44 London Street, East) • Montreal, Quebec, (1188 Dorchester Street, West)

You won't find all these Super-Coach features in even the costliest private car: Four-position easy chairs with sponge-rubber cushions; massive rubber footrests; translucent pull-down shades; directed-beam reading lights; perfected air-conditioning.

FREE! NEW CARTOON MAP

A brand new "Amazing America" Cartoon Map, with more than 100 entertaining pictures and stories, in full color. Simply mail this coupon to the nearest Greyhound Information Bureau listed above (no local address necessary).

Name _____

Address _____

City _____   HT-2

GREYHOUND

ABOVE *Jackson, Mississipi. Another of the "blue" 1930s stations, this terminal was also designed by W. M. Arrasmith, who completed it in 1937. Decommissioned several years ago, it would surely have been demolished if local architect R. Parker Adams, who used to play pinball in the station every day as a child, had not bought it and restored it to perfection.*

RIGHT *The Jackson Depot before it was decommissioned.*

have the same impact, but it still provided Greyhound with some very welcome free advertising.

When the Revenue Act of 1936 came into being, although aimed at restricting public utility holding companies, it had a direct effect on Greyhound whereby some 20 operating subsidiaries were merged and brought under the control of The Greyhound Corporation. Indeed, this can be seen to be the start of a lengthy consolidation policy which ultimately brought about the unified Greyhound system in the 1970s.

1936 also saw the beginnings of the National Trailways Bus System which, in contrast to Greyhound, was an associ-ation of independent bus companies rather than a holding company with a number of subsidiaries. Trailways, under the prompting of people like Aaron E. Greenleaf and Paul J. Neff, rapidly developed into a truly national organisation, quickly adopted a standard red and cream colour scheme for its buses and began operating a through ticketing system which the public favoured.

But without doubt, the most important event of 1936 as far as Greyhound was concerned was the arrival of the Model 719 'Super Coach' built by GM division Yellow Coach. This radical new streamlined design was to change the face of intercity bus travel forever. Thanks to the rear-mounted engine, the driver now sat ahead of the front wheels and enjoyed an unobstructed forward view. Greater passenger capacity (now up to 36) in the same overall length of vehicle came about by raising the floor above the engine level, which also allowed a capacious baggage compartment to be created in between the front and rear wheels. Extensive used of aluminium in the construction of this bus reduced the weight by two tons over previous models.

Although the Super Coach was an innovation, the principles of its design had been around for while, and some of them had already been used on earlier Greyhound buses. The outline shape was first seen on the 1927 Fageol Twin Coach, and the underfloor stowage of luggage had also been seen before a decade earlier on buses built by the American Car & Foundry Co (ACF) and on some other makes too. Even the transverse rear engine wasn't new – Dwight Austin had patented an 'angle drive' and used it on a series of Nite Coach buses he constructed for Greyhound in 1933-34 using the old Pickwick Corporation factory in Los Angeles, California.

Yellow Coach brought Dwight Austin to their Pontiac, Michigan, headquarters in 1934 and immediately took his patented drivetrain and adapted it to their own buses. Greyhound contributed towards some of the cost of the engineering development and design work, and also made

BELOW *Jackson, Tennessee. One of the most incredible examples of the old Greyhound terminals is to be found in the plantation state of Tennessee. The quiet, sleepy town of Jackson harbours a huge Art Deco station, which seems to have hardly changed since the day it was inaugurated. Completely unrestored, this is a fully working station, to which the patina of time has added a wonderful sense of character.*

ABOVE *Ever since the days when the bus went only from Hibbing to Alice, Greyhound travel has always meant much more than just getting from A to B. More than a mere transportation vehicle, the bus is ultimately a container of people, a melting pot on wheels where people of all backgrounds and colours can get to know each other. It may seem surprising, but in present day America, where everybody sometimes seems to be afraid of everybody else, the Greyhound bus is one of the last public places where total strangers will still strike up a conversation. Lonnie, photographed in Jackson at the end of a ten hour trip, told stories of life in the L.A. Projects and gave first-hand descriptions of its dangers and lack of opportunities. By the end of the trip, the whole bus was listening.*

suggestions based on their experiences as an operator. Dwight Austin is also credited with being involved with the exterior styling of the Super Coach, together with James J. St.Croix, and Orville Caesar seems to have had a major influence on behalf of Greyhound. Air conditioning was another innovation that first appeared in the Model 743 Super Coach introduced in 1937 (right), using a system called Tropic-Aire manufactured by a Greyhound subsidiary. Production of the Super Coach totalled nearly 1600 by 1939 when the design was superseded.

Inevitably, such a successful concept as the Super Coach was quickly taken up by other bus builders who produced their own versions. ACF, Kenworth, and the Fort Garry Motor Body Co. of Winnipeg, Canada (later to become Motor Coach Industries in 1940), were some of the first to copy the ideas – the rest soon followed.

The New York World's Fair, opened by President Franklin D. Roosevelt on April 30th 1939, not only generated extra passenger traffic through bus tours and charters, it also provided Greyhound and Yellow Coach with an ideal platform to introduce an improved and restyled Super Coach that became known as the 'Silversides'.

The prototype bus displayed at the World's Fair was fitted with the same 707 cu.in. (11.6 litre) gasoline engine as had been used in most of the earlier Super Coaches, but the vast majority of Silverside production buses were powered by six cylinder Detroit Diesel engines as Greyhound led the industry

in switching to this more economical method of propulsion. In 1938 it is estimated that there were only something like 200 diesel-powered buses operating in the USA; by 1948 this number had multiplied to over 18,000 – a fantastic revolution.

But, before that revolution could get into full swing, a much more cataclysmic event was to take place. On December 7, 1941, the Japanese attacked Pearl Harbor, Hawaii, and the USA entered World War Two. Production of large intercity buses was halted as the factories were turned over to armament manufacture. However, smaller urban buses were still being made under the auspices of the War Production Board, and many saw use on long distance routes.

Hundreds of old buses that had been scheduled for retirement were dragged out of the boneyards, refurbished and put back to work. Even so, overcrowding became an everyday occurrence as military personnel and civilians on essential

ABOVE *Uvalde Texas. Throughout the 1930s the Greyhound Co. was affiliated with several smaller organisations, which serviced secondary routes and operated their own terminals. This Painter terminal in Southern Texas has remained untouched for 60 years. Inside, the layout is very simple, and as you can see, the notice boards are still homemade.*

journeys filled every seat and stood packed in the aisles. Despite a vigorous camapign using the slogan 'Is This Trip Necessary?' bus passenger mileage went from 10.1 million miles in 1940, to more than double in 1942 at 21.5 million. It peaked at 27.4 million miles in 1943.

It was a difficult time for the bus operator; spare parts were hard to obtain, gasoline and tyres were rationed, and staff shortages meant longer hours. In some cases, transporting workers to shipyards and aircraft factories was taken care of by the use of converted trailers, and competing companies were forbidden from duplicating bus routes by the government for the duration of the war. The war years also saw the first female bus drivers being hired by Greyhound.

Towards the end of the conflict, in 1945, a one-time bus station ticket agent named M. E. Moore merged the Tri-State Transit Co and Bowen Motor Coaches to form the Continental Bus System Inc. based in Dallas, Texas. This marked the first time two formerly independent member companies of the Trailways system had been bought out and combined, and was the beginning of the creation of a second strong national bus system with central management control.

ABOVE *The Uvalde Depot Cafe is a rare surviving example of the coffee shops and restaurants that were often attached to Greyhound stations. In the early '40s there were almost 100 such restaurants, called Post Houses. Nowadays most have been replaced by fast food chains, but this little diner has managed to keep its original identity against all the odds.*

Washington DC. Thanks to the efforts of the Art Deco Society of Washington, this marvellous terminal has been saved and has been turned into the main lobby of a modern tower, built in 1991 by a Canadian insurance company. The original Greyhound terminal was opened in 1939 and was perhaps the most flamboyant of all the ones built by W.S.Arrasmith. The interior was even more outré than the outside, with a domed skylit ceiling, copper-edged walnut benches and a greyhound motif in the middle of the terrazzo floor. Restoration architect Hyman Myers went out of his way to use traditional materials such as flexwood, a canvas backed veneer which was used for the curved balcony. Artist John Grazier was commissioned to paint murals of buses outside national landmarks, in the spirit of the lost originals.

KINGS OF THE ROAD

Caesar, Silversides & Scott

Although Greyhound had plans to introduce a completely new type of bus after the war, it never made it into production and in 1946, Orville Caesar announced that the company had ordered a new fleet of Silversides from the GMC Truck & Coach Division of General Motors (formerly Yellow Coach – the name was changed at the end of 1942). Eventually 2,000 buses of this type with either 37 or 41 seat capacity were delivered between 1947 and 1948 and these formed the basis of the first large fleet of diesel-powered buses in the USA.

Instantly recognisable by their fluted aluminium sides, the classic Silversides (in effect, a Super Coach with different styling) featured some mechanical improvements over the pre-war buses, but were basically similar in appearance. One alteration noticed by the driver was the adoption of a column-mounted gear shifter, following the trend found in automobiles of the period.

An aborted project, a 50-seater double-decker bus known as the Highway Traveler, began in 1945 when Greyhound issued design contracts to GMC and Convair. Also referred to as the GX-1, this bus featured many ideas that were to become standard on later bus designs: air suspension, lavatory compartment, thermostatically controlled air conditioning and high-level seating to give better visibility.

Another unique idea incorporated in the design of the Highway Traveler (apparently at the insistence of Orville Caesar) was the use of two air-cooled gasoline engines. It was intended that one engine would run all the time, and the second engine could be brought into use for climbing hills, overtaking, or whenever extra power was needed. This was supposed to be more economical than running one big engine constantly, but the mechanical complication of the arrangement proved unworkable. Styled by famous designer Raymond Loewy, only one prototype Highway Traveler was built – by Greyhound itself, after GMC and Convair pulled out of the project – and it was eventually finished in the early part of 1947.

In 1948 Greyhound, who had been purchasing almost the entire output of MCI buses over the years, acquired the Winnipeg based bus and coach building company, thereby returning to the situation of having an in-house supplier for the first time since 1930.

Although the bulk of the Greyhound fleet in the late 1940s consisted of Sliversides built by GMC, it was by no means completely standardised and the company still used many

RIGHT *1947 Silversides. From a design point of view, the new GMC bus was full of surprises. The huge rear stop light was as much an advertisement as it was an effective stop signal.*

Hardly surprisingly, the war put a stop to Greyhound expansion plans, but only temporarily. Even during the course of the conflict the company kept building new buses – aptly named Victory buses – which carried thousands of military personnel to their induction centres. For obvious reasons, these were relatively basic, unreliable machines. In 1946, however, Orville Caesar was able to announce that the company had ordered 1,200 "Silversides" from the GMC Truck & Coach Division of General Motors. Once again, the new coaches were state-of-the-art in terms of design, engineering and comfort. The Silversides was a 41-seat fully air-conditioned, centrally heated bus with transverse rear-mounted 6-71 Detroit Diesel engine. (Heating and air conditioning take up a lot of space in the 'Troubleshooting Guide' issued to all drivers today: "Blowers not on – blower reset tripped – reset, left front baggage bin.") The nation's new affluence and sense of optimism was duly reflected in the Silversides' gleaming stainless steel and aluminium design.

other makes of buses. An outstanding example of these other buses was the ACF Brill, built in Philadelphia. Powered by a six cylinder 707 cu.in. Hall-Scott gasoline engine mid-mounted between the axles, ACF Brill buses were very fast and used by other lines including Trailways. One disadvantage with the ACF Brill was that, because of the engine postion, the only luggage carrying space was underneath the seats. The first ACF Brill was delivered to Virginia Stage Lines in December, 1945 and Pennsylvania Greyhound received their intial batch in January 1946. The bulk of ACF Brill buses were built between 1945

and 1950, although the bus stayed in production until 1953 and the later models came with a Cummins diesel engine.

By 1950 the bus lines carried almost 37% of intercity travellers who used public transport, and the railroads share had declined to less than 47%. The airlines were taking an increasing percentage of the market, up from 3.2% in 1942 to 14.6% in 1950, showing how they were on course to dominate the US travel scene in the decades to come.

Greyhound increased the number of all-expense tours on offer to over 200, and the selection continued to grow. The company also provided a large choice of charter services that could be used for business travel, sports events or pleasure excursions. In some advertisements, the company liked to imply that a charter bus was just like having a luxury limousine and personal chauffeur at your disposal! But the pressure was certainly already on...

As always, the little chrome greyhound was placed on the coach's nose, this time enclosed in an oval shaped motif.

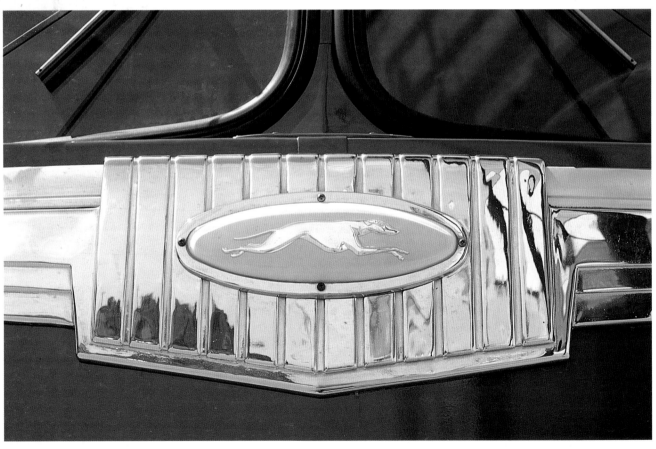

YOUR VACATION   WILL BE

Easy to Take

when you take it by GREYHOUND

It's *Easy to Find* the right schedules—Greyhound buses leave so frequently, at such convenient hours. It's *Easy to Reach* the choice vacation places, since Greyhound serves all 48 States and Canada. ● It's *Easy to Relax* in deeply-cushioned, adjustable chairs. *Easy on the Eyes* are the beauty spots, found only by Greyhound. ● *Easy to Buy* are Greyhound tickets, offering big savings on almost any trip . . . *Easy to Plan* is your outing, with the help of a friendly Greyhound agent.

William Wyan, a Greyhound driver for 30 years, at the wheel of an old Silversides.

"The seven mile bridge between Miami-Key West"

"The bus that goes to sea"

ABOVE *"The bus that goes to sea," a Silversides on its way to Key West on the famous Overseas Highway Bahia-Honda bridge.*

RIGHT *The Silversides had a new modern interior which provided the passengers with unprecedented levels of comfort. They could relax in four-position adjustable chairs stuffed with the all new "sponge rubber" foam, stretch their legs thanks to retractable rubber footrests and read their Highway Traveler magazines with the help of directional reading lights. Not surprisingly, during and after the war buses continued to be filled to capacity, enabling Greyhound to earn almost $20 million in 1946.*

ABOVE LEFT *Dallas, Texas. A vintage Silversides parked in front of the beautifully restored Dallas depot.*

BELOW LEFT *Cleveland, Ohio. As the number of passengers increased, Greyhound built bigger and bigger terminals. When the one in Cleveland was completed (1943) it was claimed to be the biggest bus station in the world. It cost a record $1,250,000 and served over three million passengers every year, thanks to its 21 loading platforms and huge curved lobby. After the War, terminals similar to the one pictured here kept being built at an ever faster rate. In 1949 alone 21 terminals, 9 garages and 7 combinations of the two were constructed.*

RIGHT *Cleveland Terminal's crowning glory. The hands may have fallen off the clock at the top of the tower, but time has yet to run out for this typical 1940s station, which remains a favourite among Greyhound travellers.*

BELOW *The Super Coaches of the 1930s and early '40s had a small, discreet greyhound painted on their flank. The new Silversides, as if to underline the company's new aggressive attitude, carried much more visible, larger and sleeker dogs running along their sides.*

59

GERONIMO'S CASTLE — GREYHOUND BUS DEPOT — BOWIE, ARIZONA   SB H1487

LEFT *Bowie, Arizona. The only tepee-shaped Greyhound terminal in existence, and surely the most bizarre bus station in the world. Extravagantly named Geronimo's Castle (the great Apache chief was apparently captured nearby) it was built in the 1940s, at a time when such vernacular buildings were springing up all over the Western United States. In its heyday the Tepee attracted many thirsty soldiers on their way to training camps in California.*

INSET *A 1945 view of the Bowie, Arizona terminal. Buses to and from Tucson, Arizona, stop there every day.*

ABOVE *Inside Geronimo's Castle. Known these days simply as the Tepee Bar, the place hasn't changed a bit. Customers are still served by a lady dressed as an Indian, and dollar bills left as tips are still used as wallpaper.*

ABOVE *Back in the 1940s, the Greyhound fleet was not completely standardised. While most coaches came from GMC, the company also bought equipment from other manufacturers. One such firm was ACF-Brill, a subsidiary of the American Car & Foundry Motors Co. of Detroit, Michigan. In 1945 they started making for Greyhound a beautifully streamlined coach, known simply as the ACF Brill. It had a six-cylinder Hall-Scott underfloor engine with optional Spicer hydraulic transmission, and was a favourite among the drivers, who loved its reliability and smooth power.*

LEFT *The rear (naturally) featured the hound.*

RIGHT *Like their GMC counterparts, the Brills had aluminium logos attached to their sides. The southeastern logo, with the added compass rose symbolizing the company's pan-continental policy, was perhaps the most beautiful of all.*

LEFT *Aerodynamic and fast, the Brill was also extremely comfortable. Thanks to fans mounted inside the ceiling ducts, its air-conditioning system was extremely effective at keeping the interior cool, even when temperatures outside were unbearably high. If the weather turned, there were heating units under the floor to convey warm air to the new, ergonomically contoured seats.*

The Highway Traveler magazine was distributed free of charge to Greyhound passengers and was the equivalent of today's "in-flight" publications. Full of (pretty good) articles on history and travel, it was published bi-monthly and had a circulation of about 500,000.

ABOVE *Kingman, Arizona. Travelling through Arizona, the bus follows old Route 66, one of the oldest – and the most famous – road in America. The Silversides painted on a wall near Kingman's railway station is a reminder of the halcyon days of the "Mother Road".*

RIGHT *Benson, Arizona. The Quarter Horse Motel, another relic from the 1940s, welcomes travellers passing through this tiny Arizona town with one of the best vintage neons of the area.*

LEFT *Old US Highway 86, going through Bowie, Arizona.*

BELOW *Highway 66 East of Kingman, Arizona.*

ABOVE *Greyhound recycling at its best: a heavily customised GMC Silversides 4104 bus patiently awaits a new owner in Bracketville, Texas.*

LEFT *Situated close to the old Greyhound terminal, the Yucca Lodge Motel in Bowie is typical of the mid 1940s. All over America motels like this one are disappearing fast, leaving the roadside to nationwide hotel chains and fast food restaurants.*

TOP *Dinosaur, Colorado. The Miner's Cafe, not far from the Dinosaur National Park, is a favourite stop for travellers. Inside this tiny diner passangers and cowboys often gather in front of the woodstove with a much needed cup of coffee. Outside, the bitter winter winds can bring temperatures down to -20C.*

ABOVE *Aluminium had of course been a reserved resource in the war years; the aluminium and steel are the essence of the Greyhound look.*

Top *Gallup, New Mexico. The Indian Capital of the USA has some of the best preserved 1940s diners and cafes. The abundance of period signs makes this one of those US towns where time seems to have stood still.*

Above *Chief Yellow Horse Trading Post, 10 miles west of the city, still attracts plenty of business. Fifty years ago it was a major Indian tourist attraction and the site of several Hollywood movie productions.*

Right *Greyhound logo, inevitably, on the Silversides rear brake light.*

PANORAMIC VIEWS

This Beautiful America…

Barely seven months of the Fifties had elapsed before events took place that would lead to the outbreak of the Korean War. President Truman declared a state of emergency on December 16, 1950 which, among other things, restricted the availability of essential materials like steel, nickel and chromium. And for the first three months of 1951 the US auto industry suffered a compulsory 20% restriction of output to conserve metal stocks for military use.

Dwight D. Eisenhower won the Republican nomination and then the 1952 presidential election and, with his running mate Richard Nixon, took over in the White House in January 1953. On July 12 1954, in Washington DC, Vice President Nixon announced a major new road building programme that would cost $50 billion, spread over the next decade. Concentrating on the construction of a network of interstate highways, in its own way this initiative would have as profound effect on the bus industry as the 'Good Roads' legislation introduced in the Federal Highway Act of 1916. Greyhound used the ever-improving freeways to introduce a number of limited and express runs which allowed cross-country passengers to complete their journey without changing buses.

But it was the unveiling of the split-level Scenicruiser bus that really put Greyhound ahead of its competitors. Taking the

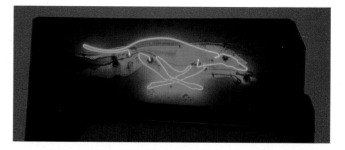

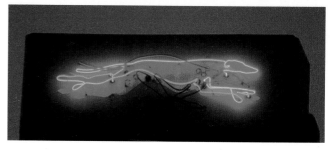

ABOVE *The last "running dog" in the country, at Evansville, Indiana.*

ill-fated Highway Traveler concept a stage further, in 1949 a prototype bus named the GX-2 was constructed by GMC in cooperation with Greyhound, using a Raymond Loewy design (Loewy was employed as a consultant by GM's head of styling Harley Earl). A three-axle configuration, stretched to 40 feet in length (instead of the normal 35 feet) with 10 passengers at the same level as the driver and 33 on the rear upper deck, the Scenicruiser was a masterpiece. Before the Scenicruiser could take to the freeways in earnest Greyhound had to set

ABOVE *In the early 1950s, as President Eisenhower's massive inter-state highway programme was beginning to transform the American landscape, the Greyhound empire was at its peak. With 6,280 buses and 90,000 miles of scheduled routes, Greyhound dominated the market and was able to think big. Very big. Its contribution to the new age of technological optimism was the world-famous Scenicruiser, a totally new kind of coach which, like the cars of the period, looked capable of inter-planetary travel. Despite the tragedy of the Korean War, the fifties was America's decade.*

OVERLEAF *1954 Scenicruiser. The revolutionary new coach was built by GMC specifically for Greyhound. It was one of the first ever bi-level buses, with 10 passengers seated on the driver level and 33 up above. The new arrangement provided increased luggage space and, most important, a fully furbished rear toilet compartment. Originally the bus was powered by two rear-mounted 4-71 Detroit Diesels with a fluid coupling connection and common propeller shaft. It suffered from unreliability until the introduction of the 220 bhp 8V-71 Detroit engines in 1961.*

out on a countrywide lobbying campaign with the GX-2 proto-type to get approval for this larger bus and make certain it would be legal for use in all states. The GX-2 also saw service on regular routes as various ideas were tried and modifica-tions carried out. In 1954, Greyhound ordered 1,000 Scenicruisers (GMC Model No. PD-4501) and the first was delivered in July of that year. In addition to air suspension and

a lavatory to make travel more comfortable for the passen-gers, the extra luggage capacity of the Scenicruiser allowed Greyhound to promote an express parcel service – which proved a major boon for outlying communities and gave the company welcome additional revenue.

Originally, all 1,000 Scenicruisers were built with dual rear-mounted four cylinder Detroit Diesel engines driving

ABOVE *The slanted windows gave the impression of speed, enhancing the sleek design of the Scenicruiser. The 90% glare-resistant glass used for the panoramic windows was developed especially for Greyhound, and there were even skylights in the roof. Teenagers could now lean back and gaze at the stars.*

RIGHT *A true child of the fifties, this was possibly the last really innovative, anything-is-possible American bus. When it covered the 3,000-mile-long intercontinental "Through Bus Schedules" the Scenicruiser was a kind of "road-plane", with reserved seat service, free pillows, radio and on board hostess. The driver used the new public address system to point out places of interest and generally keep the customers entertained. Thus the tradition of Greyhound drivers' fantastic – notorious? – sense of humour was born.*

through a fluid coupling linked to a single transmission. Although complicated, this system functioned reasonably well, but was unreliable in service, not liked and consquently the surviving 979 buses were re-equipped with a single eight cylinder Detroit Diesel engine and a Spicer 4-speed manual transmission by the Marmon-Herrington Corporation at Indianapolis, Indiana, between 1961 and 1962.

Because the Scenicruiser was exclusive to Greyhound, competitors had to look elsewhere for a bus of similar design. Continental Trailways went to the Flexible Company of Loudonville, Ohio, who came up with a split-level design called the Vistaliner. Seating either 37 or 41 passengers, the Vistaliner was a two-axle bus and only 35 feet in length and, although sold to other lines as well as Trailways, only 208 were built between 1955 and 1958.

In 1957 Trailways imported 50 Golden Eagle buses from Germany. Built by Karl Kassbohrer AG, these 40 foot long, three-axle buses seated 41 passengers at high-level and had a lavatory plus lounge area at the rear. The following year the first Silver Eagle buses – 45 seaters without any luxury amenities – were delivered, and became the standard Trailways bus. These were the first of thousands of Eagle buses bought by

Trailways over the years. In 1962 the company set up its own factory in Belgium (operated in partnership with La Brugeoise) and Bus & Car N.V. used many American components (in particular Detroit Diesel engines and transmissions) in the Eagle buses it produced. Then, in 1974, Eagle International Inc was established in Brownsville, Texas, and started assembling buses using parts imported from Belgium.

Meanwhile, Greyhound was also very much in the business of building its own buses. Late in 1963, it established an assembly plant at Pembina, North Dakota, for its subsidiary Motor Coach Industries. The MCI MC-5 bus was the first to be produced at Pembina, with running gear and interiors being added to bodies shipped from the Winnipeg factory 70 miles north across the USA/Canada border. *(Cont. p 90)*

Thanks to a unique three-axle alignment (above) and springs mounted in tension rubber shackles, the Scenicruiser ride was smoother than ever. The new air suspension system was so effective that advertisments claimed the bus "floated entirely on cushions of air". The styling retained the traditional white and blue colours, together with the stainless steel and aluminium finish. Incredibly, it wasn't until 1957 that Greyhound adopted a real live dog as a promotional device. Incongruously named 'Steverino' (because Greyhound sponsored the Steve Allen TV show at the time), her name was later changed to the far more suitable "Lady Greyhound". Wearing a jewelled tiara and collar, she made hundreds of public appearances for the company and for charity.

1954

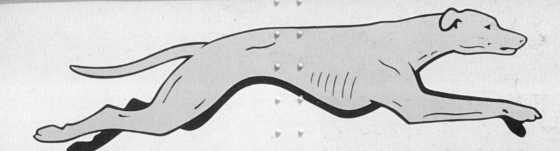

Greyhound

195

ABOVE *Plastics were everywhere. The seats, often upholstered with the mosaic patterns typical of the 50s, were adjustable and resembled those used on airplanes. The fifties would see Greyhound drivers begin making on-board announcements to passengers thanks to the installation of a speaker system, and bus hostesses were introduced to assist travellers. The decade also produced a classic slogan, the world-famous: 'Go Greyhound – And Leave The Driving To Us.'*

LEFT *San Antonio, Texas. Casual and striking at the same time, the sign advertising the San Antonio terminal is pure fifties.*

Every mile a Magnificent Mile...
every highway a strip of velvet...

Greyhound
SCENICRUISER

when you travel in the amazing new
Scenicruiser

Get ready to experience the smoothest, most thrilling travel in highway history, when you step aboard Greyhound's luxurious new *Scenicruiser!* This is the revolutionary motor coach that floats entirely on cushions of air, to give you the gentlest ride ever known—that provides panoramic sightseeing on two observation levels —offers washroom convenience, many, many other luxury features.

A great fleet of 500 *Scenicruisers* is scheduled to serve all America— scores are already in operation. And *only by Greyhound* can you travel in this motor coach of tomorrow!

GREYHOUND®

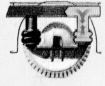

RAISED LEVEL SIGHTSEEING—Relax in a body-contoured easychair, enjoy panoramic sightseeing on four sides and overhead.

GENTLE AIR SUSPENSION RIDE

Entire coach floats on cushions of air, contained in flexible rubber-nylon bellows. Road shock and vibration are magically absorbed.

Hundreds of modern Greyhound "Highway Traveler" coaches also offer Air Suspension, huge picture windows, air conditioning.

COMPLETE WASHROOM

The *Scenicruiser* has a completely equipped washroom—with wash basin, running water, toilet, mirror, other features so convenient on longer trips.

FREE! Pleasure Map of America

Mail to Greyhound Tour Dept., 71 W. Lake Street, Chicago 1, Ill., for full-color trip-planning map—with details on 50 Greyhound Expense-Paid Tours.

Name_____

Address_____

City & State_____

Send me special information on a tour to:

_____

L-9-54

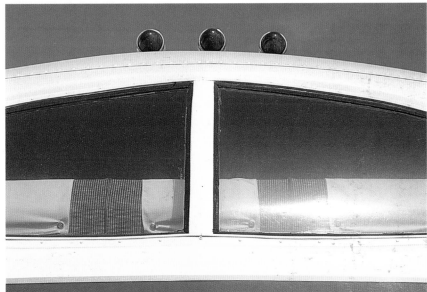

The Scenicruiser design details (above) display all the confidence and bravura that marked so much of US manufacturing in the 1950s. "It's such a comfort to go by bus – and leave the driving to us." Apart from forming an integral part of the cultural fabric of "This Wonderful America", the Greyhound company also inspired one of the best forced rhymes in popular music: "She shook his hustle, A Greyhound bus'll – take the one that got away." (Tom Waits)

RIGHT *San Antonio, Texas. One of the friendliest cities in the USA, San Antonio has one of the busiest terminals. Situated close to the famous Alamo, the depot is always teeming with people travelling to and from the Mexican city of Nuevo Laredo, only a few hours away.*

LEFT *Dallas, Texas. When the Greyhound Corporation moved its headquarters to Dallas, the city's terminal was restored and modernised. One of the most beautiful modern terminals, Dallas retains many of the elements which over the years have been used to enhance the company image.*

ABOVE *Vernal, Utah. A pink brontosaurus (nicknamed Dino) welcomes travellers to the DineAville Motel. Vernal claims to be the dinosaur capital of America, due to its proximity with the Dinosaur National Monument. Many similarly outrageous motel signs built in the post-war years have sadly disappeared.*

RIGHT *Period views of the Akron, Ohio, and Pittsburgh, Pennsylvania, terminals.*

Greyhound Bus Terminal, Akron, Ohio

STIVAS STUDIO PHOTO   OC-H649

Greyhound Bus Terminal, Pittsburgh, Pa.

For many people, the magical country that lies between New York and Los Angeles can still only be experienced directly from the front seat of a Greyhound bus. The Greyhound experience is de rigueur for any self-respecting student backpacker from Europe.

The MC-5 was very popular, particularly with operators wanting a shorter 35 foot coach. 2,255 were built, with later versions carrying A, B and C suffixes to the basic model number.

Greyhound's 50th anniversary was celebrated in 1964; to mark the event, every Greyhound bus had a broad gold stripe added to the traditional blue and white colour scheme. Once the commemoration was over, the gold stripe was replaced by a red one, and the now familiar red, white and blue design was established, still to be seen now, thirty years on.

In an effort to build an improved replacement for the spliit-level Scenicruser (by now well over ten years old) in 1967 MCI put a new prototype on the road. Called the MC-6, it was 40 feet in length with three axles and all the passengers sat at high level. The most controversial aspect of the MC-6 though, was its width. Greyhound had added six inches to the normal bus width of 96 inches to provide more passenger room and comfort – outside the legal limit in most states.

As with the Scenicruser in 1954, Greyhound tried to get the 102 inch wide bus accepted but in this instance the company failed – Congress refused to alter the maximum legal width allowed on the Interstate highway system. *(Cont. p 96)*

ABOVE The Scenicruiser may have gone, but the views are still there. The imposing New Mexico landscape unravels outside the tinted windows of a modern Americruiser 2 on its way to Truth or Consequences, the town named after a 1950s TV show.

LEFT Tucson, Arizona. The pleasant terminal interior, always busy with passengers 24 hours a day.

RIGHT When the sixties arrived, the oval logo used for years on the front of the buses became particularly popular. In Tucson it was featured at the top of the terminal's flagstaff style sign.

ABOVE *Amarillo, Texas. The Cadillac Ranch, famous celebration of the "chrome and fin" car-culture of America. It can be seen easily from buses travelling on Interstate 40 between Wildorado and Amarillo.*

LEFT *Colombus, Ohio. A driver checks his schedule while refuelling. Greyhound drivers are rightly considered to be the safest bus drivers in America.*

ABOVE *Horseshoe Café, US 80, Arizona.*

RIGHT *Pictures of horses, blueberry pies and the old Wurlitzer are what make the Horseshoe Café a favourite among Greyhound travellers.*

Above *Bus sign at Colombus, Ohio.*

Right *In 1948 Greyhound acquired Motor Coach Industries, manufacturers of bus body shells, and in 1963 started making their own buses at plants in Pembina, North Dakota and Winnipeg, Canada. The first Greyhound MCI bus was the 39-passenger MC-5, followed - by the experimental MC6 and then, in 1968, the 6 wheeled 47-passenger MC-7, shown here.*

Having already built 100 of these so-called 'Supercruiser" buses, powered by a huge V12 diesel engine in place of the usual V8, Greyhound was forced to limit their use to routes where state laws permitted wider buses or where special permission was granted. Fifteen MC-6 buses spent all their working life in Canada, the remaining 85 were used for a time on the east coast, but ended up in California.

The twelve cyclinder engine in the west coast buses were removed in 1977 and replaced by Detroit Diesel V8s and Allison automatic transmissions (originally the MC-6 had a manual transmission) and were sold off from Greyhound service in 1980 – an expensive gamble for the company to lose.

Facing these difficulties with the MC-6, MCI introduced the MC-7 in 1968. Of standard 96 inches width, this forty foot long, three axle bus was based on the shorter MC-5 and equipped with a conventional drivetrain. The MC-7, sometimes called the "Super 7 Scenicruiser", remained in production until 1973, by when 2,550 had been produced.

ABOVE *Guess what's on the front?*

BELOW *Back to basics with the MC-7, following MC-6 problems, with conventional drivetrain.*

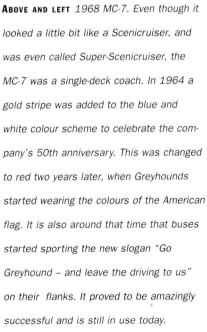

ABOVE AND LEFT *1968 MC-7. Even though it looked a little bit like a Scenicruiser, and was even called Super-Scenicruiser, the MC-7 was a single-deck coach. In 1964 a gold stripe was added to the blue and white colour scheme to celebrate the company's 50th anniversary. This was changed to red two years later, when Greyhounds started wearing the colours of the American flag. It is also around that time that buses started sporting the new slogan "Go Greyhound – and leave the driving to us" on their flanks. It proved to be amazingly successful and is still in use today.*

GOING GREYHOUND
The Red, White & Blue

For America, the 1970s were of course a turbulent decade: as if you needed reminding of some of the grimmer highlights, the Vietnam War, Watergate, gasoline shortages caused by the oil embargo in 1973, and the nuclear disaster at Three Mile Island in 1979. In the ten years from 1970 to 1980 the population of the USA rose from 203 million to 226 million, but the bus companies were facing increasing competition for passenger traffic – mainly from the private automobile, but also from the airlines over the longer distances.

At the start of the Seventies, in 1971 to be precise, Greyhound moved its corporate headquarters from Chicago to Phoenix, Arizona, citing in its company literature 'the need for more spacious facilities' as the reason for the relocation. This was also the year that Amtrak, the National Railroad Passenger Corporation began operations, but the day of the train as the premier mass passenger carrier had long passed. Mostly, headlines about buses in the '70s were associated with 'busing' students in order to integrate American schools. Violence and rioting were commonplace when busing took place and the buses usually required armed police escorts. The segregation in education debate continued right through the 1970s and beyond, but the busing issue gradually faded from prominence.

On a more positive note, Greyhound introduced the 'Ameripass' in 1972. This scheme offered unlimited travel by bus in the USA and Canada over a weekly or monthly period for a single special payment which equated to a huge discount

Tucson, Arizona. Another stop, another Coke. Getting ready for yet another night on the bus.

ABOVE *In 1973 Greyhound introduced the MC-8, the last coach with Scenicruiser-type slanting windows. Six years later came the MC9. This no-nonsense, comfortable coach proved to be one of the best workhorses the company ever had, so much so that it is still widely used today.*

on the regular fares charged. The 1970s also saw the phasing out the use of on-board hostesses that had been introduced by Greyhound some twenty years earlier.

Towards the end of the decade, Greyhound introduced the MCI MC-9 bus, in 1979. In the automobile industry, the MC-9 would probably be referred to as a face-lift of the MC-8, as it retained most of the mechanical components and layout of the earlier model but with a revised body design. Increased glass area, plus the elimination of the slanting window panels on either side, and a higher windshield as the dip in the roof line above the driver was done away with, are the main identifying features of the MC-9 when compared to the MC-8. Greyhound mainly used the MC-9 in a 43-passenger configuration, and the overall dimensions of 40 feet in length and

width of 96 inches remained. Many other bus operators also bought MC-9 buses and well over 9,000 were produced as manufacturing continued into the late 1980s.

In fact, the MC-9 was so popular that it was continually being re-ordered – even by Greyhound – long after it would normally have been replaced by a newer version. A new MCI bus (and a new model designation), the 102A3, would become available in October 1985, but we're getting a little ahead of ourselves.

By 1979, through acquisitions, mergers and diversification, The Greyhound Corporation listed its activities as: meat and poultry packers, bus transportation, soap products, food, financial services and pharmaceuticals. One of its most famous brand names – Dial soap – would turn out to have an inordinately significant part to play in the future of the Greyhound organisation.

Problems started for Greyhound in 1978 with the deregulation of the airlines, followed by freight in 1980 and buses in 1982. Then came a bitterly divisive strike by Greyhound workers in 1983 – by the end of all that the company had lost

ABOVE *Greyhound drivers do a lot more than deliver passengers to their destinations. On the road they point out places of interest, historical markers and even the local wildlife. Their jokes are legendary, if not always new. Many experienced drivers like Jim Burgos, photographed on the road in Colorado, have rejoined the company after the bitterly divisive strike. The badges on this driver's uniform are proof of thirty years of accident-free driving.*

ABOVE RIGHT *Lordsburgh, New Mexico.*

nearly half of its customers and shed the same percentage of employees. Troubled times indeed.

Over the next few years things were to get even worse. In December 1986, a group of Dallas, Texas, investors offered a $350 million leveraged buyout deal to purchase Greyhound

Lines from The Greyhound Corporation of Phoenix, Arizona, and created a new company. The GLI Holding Co, headed by Fred Currey, assumed control of Greyhound Lines in March 1987 and moved the company's headquarters to Dallas. For a time, the company's fortunes seemed to be heading in the right direction, particularly when only four months later, in July 1987, Greyhound bought up its great rival Trailways Lines Inc, the largest member of the National Trailways Bus Systerm. With this move Greyhound established itself as the only nationwide provider of intercity bus transportation services.

ABOVE *Hope, Arkansas. Outside the station.*

BELOW *Reflections in the windows of a California station.*

RIGHT *Ozona, Texas. Passengers look for shelter from the midday sun.*

OVERLEAF *Water towers silhouetted against a bloodred Sonoran sunset indicate the imminent arrival at yet another small town station.*

Meanwhile, The Greyhound Corporation acquired the production rights of the RTS transit bus from General Motors in January 1987. Using its subsidiary, Transportation Manufacturing Corporation in Roswell, New Mexico, Greyhound started producing the RTS by obtaining bodies from GM's factory in Pontiac, Michigan, but by September the buses were being built entirely in-house.

By now, the MCI 102A3 bus was in service and this vehicle is notable because of its unusual shape, which is not always apparent from most photographs. It is 102 inches in width (harking back to the MC-6), but only across the passenger section – the front and windshield are still at the old 96 inch width and the driver's compartment body sides taper outwards at a 5.5 degree angle. The wider 102A3 was immediately successful and thanks to the increasing number of states allowing the bigger bus access to the Interstate highways (102 inch wide buses and trucks were legal in all US states by 1990) it soon became an industry standard.

But all was not well at Greyhound, and in March 1990, following unsuccessful contract renewal negotiations, just about all the company's bus drivers, clerical workers and mechanics represented by the Amalgamated Transit Union (ATU) went on strike. Although Greyhound continued to operate by hiring replacement drivers as quickly as possible, and most of the

ABOVE *Memphis, Tennessee. The station is very close to the Sun Records studios, where Elvis cut his first singles. The Denny's restaurant across the road advertises itself with a cautious "The King probably ate here" neon.*

striking workers (apart from the drivers) returned to work, the loss of revenue and extra expenses incurred by the strike exhausted the company's cash resources. In June 1990, Greyhound filed a voluntary petition under Chapter 11 of the United States Bankruptcy Code.

A reorganisation plan was formulated and Greyhound emerged from bankruptcy on October 31, 1991 with Frank J. Schmieder as President and Chief Executive Officer. However, it seems that Frank Schmieder regarded the operation of a bus company as being the same as running an airline and tried to use the same management techniques. Critics also said he employed people in key positions who did not understand the bus industry, getting rid of experienced personnel who had spent years working for Greyhound. At this time

Greyhound withdrew from the National Trailways Bus System, thereby giving up the right to use the Trailways name.

It was also in 1991 that The Greyhound Corporation changed its name to The Dial Corporation – reasoning that the familiar and profitable soap brand provided a better corporate image than the troubled bus company. However, despite the change of name, Dial continued to own much of the property used by Greyhound Lines Inc. which it leased to the bus company and kept control of Greyhound of Canada. Dial also retained Motor Coach Industries as a subsidiary (renamed Motor Coach Industries International in 1993) with a contract which stated that Greyhound Lines must buy at least 75% of its new buses from MCII until March 1997.

The 1990 strike had seen the number of passengers carried by Greyhound in that year drop to 15.7 million from 22 million in 1989. By the end of 1992 that figure had increased slightly to 16.2 million, but it was still well below the '89 level.

1993 turned out to be another traumatic year for Greyhound as management tried to implement some radical changes to the organisation. The most notorious of these was the introduction of seat reservations in the same manner as the airlines. This was something completely new to Greyhound customers – ever since intercity bus travel had begun, passengers just turned up at the terminal and paid their fare on the day they wanted to travel. Traditionally, if the scheduled bus was full, the company would lay on another bus to make sure the extra passengers got to their destination. The idea of booking a seat two weeks in advance took the spontaneity out of bus travel.

The software for the new computerised ticket reservation system had been developed internally (at great expense) by Greyhound and was given the grandiose name of Transportation Reservation Itinerary Planning System (TRIPS). But, when introduced in August 1993, the system failed to cope with the demand, resulting in long queues and aggravating delays at the terminals. Not surprisingly, business suffered and the number of passengers carried by Greyhound that year dropped to 15.4 million with the company recording another hefty loss.

There were a couple of bright spots amid the gloom. In order to upgrade its fleet Greyhound ordered 518 new buses in 1993 – most of these being MC-12 models, an improved version of the MC-9. And, in May 1993, the company reached a settlement with the ATU – ending the three-year-long dispute – agreeing to recall 800 striking drivers. There was still the matter of back pay and the union had launched a law suit with the National Labor Relations Board claiming $143 million, which the company contested.

In order to attempt to reverse the trend initiated by TRIPS,

BELOW *Memphis, Tennessee. Thanks to an extremely efficient maintenance system, Greyhound buses are kept on the road longer than ever. On average each bus covers 125,000 miles every year.*

ABOVE *El Paso, Texas. This modern terminal, always packed with people waiting to cross the border, retains the traditional adobe look of the Southwest.*

Greyhound mounted an aggressive marketing campaign and offered substantial discounts on fares. It also revised its ideas on seat reservations and stopped taking them over the phone while the system was upgraded (TRIPS was reopened in January 1994). Passengers returned, it's true, but the discounted ticket prices meant revenue was still well down on expectations. Saddled with long-term debts of $291 million, Greyhound offered 4.7 million shares of common stock to the public in May 1993, generating $93 million in proceeds which was primarily used to purchase new buses. In March 1994, 151 new buses were ordered from MCI at a cost of $34.8 million; delivery was completed by September the same year.

Beginning in 1994, virtually all of Greyhound's dispatching activities were managed from the Central Dispatch Office using an automated scheduling system called Bus Operations Support System (BOSS). Designed to eliminate certain operational problems, BOSS enabled drivers to be informed of their assignments several days in advance, instead of when they arrived at the depot.

Other factors were also combining to create further problems at this time. The Greyhound management decided to compete against, rather than co-operate with, regional bus lines and started placing passengers on Greyhound buses where before they had used the local services which were often more efficient. In addition, where other bus companies shared the use of the Greyhound depot, they suddenly found their lease payments increased significantly. As a result, many of these bus companies stopped using the Greyhound facilities and, once again, the travelling public suffered more inconvenience.

Its no wonder then, that Greyhound's fortunes continued to decline and Frank Schmieder was to resign in August 1994. In September the company was yet again teetering on the brink of bankruptcy. Following some intense negotiations, on 13 October 1994 Greyhound entered into a new $35 million credit facility with the Foothill Capital Corporation, which replaced the company's previous bank facility.

On November 11 1994, the financial restructuring of Greyhound was agreed to by bond holders and Craig R. Lentzsch took over as President and Chief Executive Officer four days later. Lentzsch had previously been the Executive Vice President and Chief Financial Officer of Motor Coach Industries – at last, a bus person was back in the driving seat!

The number of passengers carried by Greyhound in 1994 fell to 14.9 million, but the signs for the future look promising. Lentzsch stated recently that there would be no profit in

RIGHT *Fort Stockton, Texas. Coaches travelling through the border country near Mexico are often stopped by the US Border Patrol, always on the lookout for illegal immigrants. In the great melting pot, the officers who carry out these searches are often of course the sons of immigrants themselves.*

ABOVE Sleep is a valuable commodity on the long intercontinental routes. Here, a man from Southern Mexico tries to sleep through a fuel stop in Texas, while a relief driver (top) takes a well earned rest in Southern California.

ABOVE Despite the inevitable contraction of the bus industry under the onslaught of domestic flights and auto ownership, Greyhound is still an important part of the infrastructure of America today, just as it was in the 1940s. What is remarkable is not the amount that has been lost, but just how much has survived. The street furniture and cars date the picture, not the station itself, nor, if you look quickly, the bus.

1995, but prospects for '96 were looking good. Today Greyhound operates approximately 215 million miles of regularly scheduled services to more than 2,500 destinations across 48 US states. The company also has two subsidiary bus lines – Texas, New Mexico, and Oklahoma Coaches Inc and Vermont Transit Co Inc.

Greyhound has something like 10,500 employees, including 3,500 drivers, who operate a fleet of nearly 2,000 buses. The average age of a 47-seat Greyhound bus is approximately 7 years and it will cover 125,000 miles in a year.

The immediate survival of Greyhound seems to be reasonably secure, but what of the future? The lucrative parcel delivery service has been hit in recent years by the upsurge in competition from other carriers offering an express or overnight service and Greyhound is now concentrating on local deliveries of under 400 miles. The package express part of the business now contributes less than 7% of Greyhound's annual revenue (charters account for only 1%). Competition for passengers is fiercer than ever with regional airlines offering big discounts to tempt people on board (cont p 122)

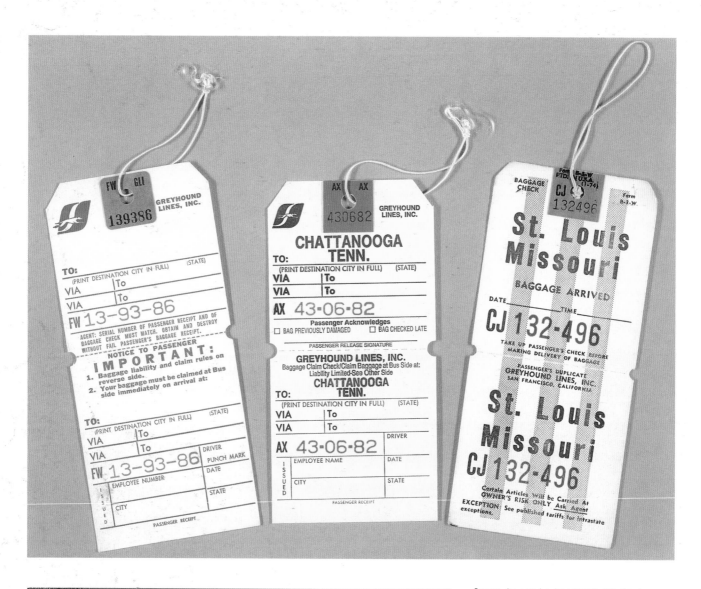

ABOVE *As can be imagined, this book involved an awful lot of baggage checks.*
LEFT *New Mexico.*
RIGHT *Two-hundred-year-old saguaros stand guard on the verges of a secondary Arizona Highway.*

ABOVE *Homestead, Florida. Still recovering from the devastation caused by Hurricane Andrew in 1992.*

RIGHT *A late winter blizzard welcomes an Americruiser 2 to Steamboat Springs, Colorado.*

ABOVE *Baby Cody, 4 months old, enjoys the view from the front seat of an Americruiser travelling through the Ohio plains. Many babies have actually been born on Greyhound buses, with drivers often having to assist with the delivery.*

ABOVE *Self-defence inside the Sonora, Texas terminal.*

RIGHT *Carl Eric Wickman's dream finally became a reality in 1987, when Greyhound Lines Inc. purchased Trailways Lines and became the only intercity bus carrier in the country. As part of the deal the company inherited many Eagles A3 buses, which were quickly converted to Greyhound colours. Some Eagles are still in use, providing efficient and comfortable service thanks to their aerodynamic body and Torsilastic suspension system. But the Eagle has never really found a place in the hearts of Greyhound aficionados. Maybe it's the large glass area, maybe it's the inner-city style doors, but for most people the Eagle somehow just isn't a Greyhound.*

ABOVE *Miami, Florida. Since 1972, when the Ameripass was intro-duced, foreign tourists have been an important source of income for Greyhound. Yukiko Kubo, from Hokaido in Japan, celebrates at the end of a long vacation on the road.*

RIGHT *An Americruiser 2 picks up passengers in Utah. On rural roads like this, flagging down the bus is a pleasant antidote to creeping agoraphobia!*

and private automobiles are being used for longer journeys more than ever before. It isn't going to be an easy ride into the next century.

Even so, it seems unthinkable that the famous 'running dog' logo and those gleaming silver-sided Americruisers could ever disappear from the USA highways – the Greyhound bus has rightly become established as an essential part of the American way of life; long may it remain so.

ABOVE *"Board a Greyhound in Pittsburgh"
sang Paul Simon, and leave the past
behind. For Eddie Conner from Virginia, a
new life in Arizona is only two days and two
nights away.*

RIGHT *The MC-12 is the latest coach made
by Motor Coach Industries for Greyhound.
Mechanically similar to the MC-9, but much
more aerodynamic. The new bus retains all
the traditional Greyhound trademarks:
small glass area, silver sides and white,
blue and red paintwork. The image that has
turned the Greyhound into an American
classic.*

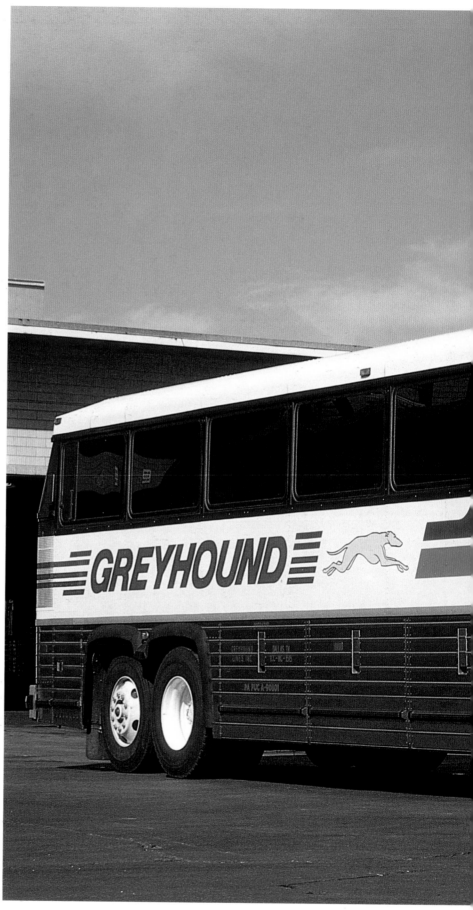

VEHICLE SPECIFICATIONS

HUPMOBILE
Year: 1914
Model: Model 32 Touring Car
Engine: 32 hp, 4 cylinder gasoline
Wheelbase: 106 inches
Seating: 7 (or as many as could be crammed aboard!)

MACK
Year: 1931
Model: BC
Engine: 6 cylinder gasoline
Wheelbase: 233 inches
Seating: 29

YELLOW COACH
Year: 1937
Model: Model 743 Super Coach
Engine: 6 cylinder GMC 707 cu.in. gasoline
Wheelbase: 245 inches
Length: 33 feet
Width: 96 inches
Height: 117 inches
Seating: 36

GMC TRUCK & COACH DIVISION
Year: 1947
Model: PD-3751 'Silversides'
Engine: 6 cylinder, 200 hp, Detroit Diesel 6-71
Wheelbase: 264 inches
Length: 35 feet
Width: 96 inches
Height: 118 inches
Seating: 37

ACF BRILL
Year: 1948
Model: IC-41
Engine: 6 cylinder, Hall-Scott 190-2 gasoline
Wheelbase: 270 inches
Length: 35 feet
Width: 96 inches
Seating: 37
Aisle width: 14 inches

GMC TRUCK & COACH DIVISION
Year: 1954
Model: PD-4501 Scenicruiser
Engine: Two Detroit Diesel 4-71 (rebuilt with single Detroit Diesel 6-71)
Wheelbase: 261 inches
Length: 40 feet
Width: 96 inches
Height: 134 inches
Seating: 43
Luggage capacity: 344 cu.ft.
Aisle width: 14 inches

MOTOR COACH INDUSTRIES
Year: 1964
Model: MC-5
Engine: 8 cylinder Detroit Diesel 8V-71
Wheelbase: 261 inches
Length: 35 feet
Width: 96 inches
Height: 120 inches
Seating: 39-45
Luggage capacity: 212 cu.ft.
Aisle width: 14 inches

MOTOR COACH INDUSTRIES
Year: 1968
Model: MC-7 'Super 7 Scenicruiser'
Engine: 8 cylinder, 252 hp Detroit Diesel 8V-71
Wheelbase: 285 inches
Length: 40 feet
Width: 96 inches
Height: 129 inches
Seating: 43-49
Luggage capacity: 325 cu.ft.
Aisle width: 14 inches

MOTOR COACH INDUSTRIES
Built by Transportation Manufacturing Corporation
Year: 1973
Model: MC-8 'Americruiser'
Engine: 8 cylinder, Detroit Diesel 8V-71C
Wheelbase: 285 inches
Length: 40 feet
Width: 96 inches
Height: 132 inches
Seating: 43/47
Luggage capacity: 300 cu.ft.
Aisle width: 14 inches
Gross Vehicle Weight: 36,500 lbs
Safe Operating Range: 750 miles

MOTOR COACH INDUSTRIES (TMC)
Year: 1980
Model: MC-9 'Americruiser 2'
Engine: 6 cylinder, Detroit Diesel 6V-92TA
Wheelbase: 285 inches
Length: 40 feet
Width: 96 inches
Height: 132 inches
Seating: 43/47
Luggage capacity: 300 cu.ft.
Aisle width: 14 inches
Gross Vehicle Weight: 36,500 lbs
Safe Operating Range: 750 miles

MOTOR COACH INDUSTRIES (TMC)
Year: 1985
Model: TMC-102A3
Engine: 6 cylinder, Detroit Diesel 6V-92TA
Wheelbase: 285 inches
Length: 40 feet, 4.25 inches
Width: 102 inches
Height: 135 inches
Seating: 47
Luggage capacity: 362 cu.ft.
Aisle width: 14 inches
Gross Vehicle Weight: 37,800 lbs
Safe Operating Range: 700 miles

MOTOR COACH INDUSTRIES
Year: 1993
Model: MC-12
Engine: 6 cylinder, Detroit Diesel
Wheelbase: 285 inches
Length: 40 feet
Width: 96 inches
Height: 132 inches
Seating: 47
Aisle width: 14 inches

GREYHOUND BUS PASSENGER PROFILE

(Taken from a 1992 On-Board Passenger Survey conducted by Greyhound)

- 56.5% of passengers are female, 43.5% male.
- Over 41% of passengers are aged between 18 and 34.
- Singles predominate – over 38% of passengers have never married, and nearly 29% are either divorced, separated or widowed.
- Most people travel alone (almost 73%) with couples the next biggest group (25%).
- 21% are retired, 13% are students and there are 2% military personnel.
- Most passengers make between one and three trips by Greyhound of over 50 miles each year (53%).
- 23% of passengers have never taken an airline flight.
- The majority of passengers get to the bus terminal by car (58%), while 33% arrive on another bus, the subway or a taxi, and only 6% walk.

LEFT *A Greyhound approaches a small town station. This image, conjured up time and time again by advertisers selling a feel for old time America, is becoming rarer. Market pressures are forcing the closure of many secondary routes and the famous Greyhound web that kept America's communities together is embattled – but fighting back.*

OVERLEAF *As another scorching day nears its end Raul Pena, driver with some 37 years of Greyhound experience, salutes a colleague going in the opposite direction on US 90 between Laredo and El Paso.*

Bury my body
down the Highway side

So my ole evil spirit
can get a Greyhound bus
and ride.

The blues of Robert Johnson, 1936.